GREAT MEATLESS MEALS

Frances Moore Lappé
and
Ellen Buchman Ewald

BALLANTINE BOOKS • NEW YORK

ISBN 0-345-29501-3

Manufactured in the United States of America

Cover photo by Laszlo

First Edition: May, 1974
Third Printing: March 1981

Contents

Introduction

The chances are that you have bought this book because you are interested in meatless meals. Although you may not be a vegetarian by conviction, you are, like everyone else in these times of soaring meat prices, being forced to think in terms of alternatives to animal foods. At the same time, you may be worried that without that steak, chop, or slice of roast pork, your family isn't getting enough protein.

To help reassure you on this score, let's review some of the facts about protein. We know that we need protein to live, and that in order to support our body's vital processes we must renew part of our supply of protein each day. The question is: What kind and how much?

When we talk about protein supply, we're really talking about two things: the *quantity* of protein in a given food, and also its *quality*—that is, the degree to which the body can make use of it. The proteins our bodies use are made up of twenty-two amino acids, in varying combinations. Eight of these, called "the eight essential amino acids" (or EEAs), cannot be snythesized by the body, but must be obtained from outside sources. And these EEAs are needed simultaneously, in the right proportions, to carry out protein synthesis. If one amino acid is even partially missing from the pattern, the use of all the others for protein synthesis is reduced proportionately.

Every food we eat can be rated in terms of how well its amino acid pattern matches the pattern required by the human body. This "biological value," plus the actual digestibility of the food, gives us its Net Protein

Utilization, or NPU, which is the actual protein available to the body after it has been consumed.

It is the NPU that is important in working out an adequate protein diet. Of all foods the egg has the particular amino acid pattern that most closely matches that of the human body and that is highest in terms of its net protein utilization. On a descending scale, milk, fish, and cheese all come *before* meat in terms of their quality rating.

When judging protein from the point of view of *quantity,* plants, particularly in their processed forms, rank highest, but unfortunately too little is used efficiently by the body. Thus, high-quantity protein often goes with low quality of absorption. Soybean flour is highest on the protein-quantity scale, with over 40 percent protein; certain cheeses, such as Parmesan, follow; next come meat, dried beans, peas, and lentils, in that order; grains, eggs, and milk are at the bottom of the scale. The bottom in quantity is well up toward the top in quality of protein absorption.

At first it would seem that in spite of their high quantity rating, the NPU of plant foods was too low to be of much value as an alternative to a meat diet. Not so. The answer lies in a process of matching one kind of plant food with another, known as "complementarity." In certain combinations of plant foods the strengths or weaknesses of the amino acid patterns are offset one by the other. For instance, beans usually have an abundance of lysine, but are deficient mainly in the sulphur-containing amino acids. Wheat, on the other hand, is deficient in lysine, but is abundant in sulphur-bearing amino acids. By combining the two in proper proportion, the protein availability is increased by 33 percent over what we would get by eating the foods separately. Other high-protein combinations are rice with beans, milk, or peanuts; cornmeal and soy; peanuts and sunflower seeds; whole wheat bread and cheese. Such protein mixes do not result in a perfect protein that is fully utilizable by the body (only the egg comes close to such perfection), but they can increase the protein quality as much as 50 percent above the average of the items if eaten separately, and, what is truly significant, in many instances will surpass the NPU of meat. A varied plant protein diet, supplemented with dairy products and eggs, will also surpass meat in providing some of the other basic nutrients.

To get back to the second part of our question: How much protein? Our minimum protein needs are based on pounds of body weight, the kind of protein consumed, and its NPU. According to *Diet for a Small Planet,** we need 0.28 grams of usable protein per pound of body weight per day. Multiplying 0.28 by 154 (the weight of the average male), we get a daily protein requirement of 43.1 grams of usable protein. For the average female (weighing 128 pounds), the requirement is 35.8 grams a day. You can calculate your own exact daily requirement by multiplying your weight by 0.28.

In any discussion of protein requirements it is important to know that the protein data on most nutrition charts is based on *total* protein and fails to take into consideration the exact amount of *usable* protein in a given food. Research to determine NPU scores of food proteins is still rudimentary, and many plant foods have not been tested. However, even with rough estimates of protein quality we are on sounder ground than if our calculations were based on total protein, when anywhere from 5 to 70 percent of this total is not usable by the body. For a more detailed discussion of complementarity and sources and amounts of usable nonmeat protein, see *Diet for a Small Planet* and *Recipes for a Small Planet.*†

**Diet for a Small Planet,* by Frances Moore Lappé (New York: Ballantine Books; 1971).
†*Recipes for a Small Planet,* by Ellen Buchman Ewald (New York: Ballantine Books; 1973).

The menus that follow are based on a nonmeat diet, and adhere to the theory of protein complementarity by combining different plant sources, or nonmeat animal protein sources with plant sources, in the same meal. In each recipe the approximate number of grams of usable protein in a single portion (average serving) is given, as well as the percentage of the daily protein allowance a single portion provides for the average man (weighing 154 pounds), and the average woman (weighing 128 pounds).

Where simple salads or fresh fruits are suggested as an addition to a meal, recipes are not provided, but when a salad contributes a significant amount of usable protein the specific recipe is given. All grains, seeds, nuts, etc., referred to in the recipes are readily obtainable at the many health food stores now available all across the country.

Great
Meatless
Meals

1

Barley and Yogurt Soup

Easy and Elegant Cheese Soufflé

Green Salad

Chocolate–Peanut Pudding

Barley and Yogurt Soup

about 2½ quarts

**1 cup = approx. 6 grams of usable protein
13% to 16% of average daily protein need**

This is a very rich soup that gets thicker and thicker as it cools. You might use leftover soup as a vegetable sauce seasoned with cayenne or curry.

A small serving wouldn't be too rich for a first course, especially followed by the light Easy and Elegant Cheese Soufflé. But you could make a complete meal with a couple of bowls of this soup and a big salad.

1 quart cold water
2 cups yogurt
4 eggs
2 tbsp whole wheat flour
1½ cups raw barley, cooked

2 tbsp or more chopped onion
2 tbsp butter
2–3 tsp salt
2 tbsp chopped fresh green herbs, such as parsley, coriander, or chives

Stir the yogurt into the quart of cold water in a large mixing bowl. Set aside.

Beat the eggs in a large saucepan or soup pot and whisk the flour into them gradually; then whisk in the yogurt mixture.

Put the pot over a high flame; don't let it boil, but keep it simmering until it thickens slightly. Stir or whisk often.

Stir in the cooked barley, onions, butter, and salt. Sprinkle with the fresh herbs just before serving.

Easy and Elegant Cheese Soufflé

5 portions

**1 portion = approx. 20 grams of usable protein
46% to 56% of average daily protein need**

3 cups grated cheese
4–6 slices bread
2 cups milk or 1½ cups
milk and ½ cup liquor
(wine or vermouth)
3 eggs, beaten

½ tsp salt
½ tsp Worcestershire
sauce
½ tsp thyme
½ tsp dry mustard
pepper

Layer the cheese and bread in an oiled baking dish, starting with the bread. Pour over it the milk or milk mixture. Beat, with the eggs, the salt and remaining ingredients and pour this over the bread mixture also. Let stand for 30 minutes. Bake at 350°F for 1 hour in a pan of hot water.

This dish sounds so very easy and homey, but it is truly elegant. When you take it out of the oven, you yourself won't believe how simply it was made. In a deep dish it has the appearance of a soufflé; in a shallow dish it resembles a quiche.

Cheeses

Chocolate–Peanut Pudding

6 portions

**1 portion = approx. 11 grams of usable protein
24% to 29% of average daily protein need**

Real pudding that is nothing like any instant you
might buy—delicious and nutritious, too.

1 ounce unsweetened
baking chocolate
½ cup crunchy peanut
butter
¼–½ cup honey

2 cups milk
2 eggs, beaten and at
room temperature
¼–½ cup raisins
(optional)
½ tsp vanilla

Melt the chocolate in the top of a double boiler; stir
in the peanut butter and honey to make a nice thick goo.

Stir in the milk and beat with a wire whisk until the
mixture is blended and very warm.

Add ½ cup of the liquid to the beaten eggs; mix well
and return them to the double boiler. Stir in the raisins.

Cook the mixture in the double boiler until it is thick,
like a custard or cream sauce—about 5 minutes.

Stir in the vanilla, pour into custard cups or one
serving dish, and chill several hours.

2

Tostadas

Cucumber and Tomato Slices
with Yogurt Dressing

Sesame Dream Bars

Tostadas

6 portions

2 tostadas = approx. 11 grams of usable protein
26% to 31% of average daily protein need

Sauce:

6 medium tomatoes, seeded and chopped
1 cup finely chopped onions
2 tsp dried oregano
½ tsp minced garlic
1 tsp honey
1 tsp salt
½ cup red wine vinegar

Combine these ingredients in a small bowl. Mix thoroughly and set aside.

Frijoles Refritos:

1½ cups dry kidney beans
1 cup chopped onions
2 medium tomatoes, chopped, or 2/3 cup canned
½ tsp minced garlic
1 tsp chili powder
pinch cayenne
5 cups water or stock
1 tsp salt

Soak the beans overnight, drain, then cook them with ½ cup of the onions, ¼ cup of tomatoes, ¼ teaspoon of the garlic, the chili, cayenne, and 5 cups of water. When they are tender add the 1 teaspoon salt.

In a large frying pan, heat some oil and sauté the remaining onions and garlic until the onions are transparent. Add the tomatoes and cook 3 minutes. Mash ¼ cup of beans into the mixture with a fork. Continue mashing and adding the beans by quarter cups. Cook about 10 minutes more, then cover the pan to keep the frijoles warm.

Dressing:
1/4 cup olive oil

2 tbsp red wine vinegar

1/4 tsp salt

3 cups shredded iceberg lettuce

Combine the dressing ingredients and mix them together well. Drop the lettuce into the mixture and toss to coat it well.

Tortillas:
1 dozen corn tortillas

oil for frying

Fry each tortilla in oil and drain on paper towels. (Fry about 1/2 minute per side.)

To assemble the tostadas:
1 cup chopped onions

1/2 cup grated Parmesan cheese

Place 1 or 2 tortillas on a plate, and spread each one with 1/3 cup refried beans. Top with 1/4 cup lettuce, some chopped onions, tomato sauce, and 2 tablespoons grated cheese.

This recipe sounds like a lot of work, but most of the combinations can be made ahead of time and then quickly assembled for a delicious meal either by you or by your guests at the table.

Sesame Dream Bars

2 dozen

1 bar = approx. 2 grams of usable protein
5% to 6% of average daily protein need

Cookie base:
1/2 cup softened butter
1/2 cup honey
1 1/4 cups whole wheat flour
1/4 cup soy flour

Top layer:
2 eggs

3/4 cup honey or brown sugar
1 tsp vanilla
1/4 cup whole wheat flour
1/4 tsp salt
1/2 tsp baking powder
1/2 cup shredded coconut, unsweetened
1/4–1/2 cup sesame seeds

Cream the butter, add the 1/2 cup honey, and continue creaming the mixture until it is very light and fluffy. Add the 1 1/4 cups whole wheat flour and 1/4 cup soy flour, and blend well. Spread the mixture in an oiled 13x9x2-inch pan (a smaller pan will give you a cakey bar) and bake at 350°F for 15 to 20 minutes, or until firm and just beginning to brown. Cool 5 minutes before adding top layer.

For the top layer, beat eggs until light, then beat in honey (or brown sugar) and vanilla. Blend in the 1/4 cup whole wheat flour, salt, and baking powder. Stir in the coconut and sesame seeds. Spread in an even layer over hot cookie base. Return to oven and bake 20 minutes more. Allow the cake to cool for about 30 minutes before cutting into squares.

3

Spinach Casserole

Three-Bean Salad

Pineapple–Corn Muffins

Spinach Casserole

4 portions

**1 portion = approx. 10 grams of usable protein
23% to 28% of average daily protein need**

¾ cup raw brown rice,
 cooked
½ cup grated cheddar
 cheese
2 eggs, beaten
2 tbsp chopped parsley

½ tsp salt
¼ tsp pepper
1 pound fresh spinach,
 chopped
2 tbsp wheat germ
1 tbsp melted butter

Combine the cooked rice and the cheese. Combine the eggs, parsley, salt, and pepper. Add the two mixtures together and stir in the raw spinach. Pour into an oiled casserole. Top with wheat germ that has been mixed with the melted butter. Bake in a 350°F oven for 35 minutes.

Spinach, Onion, Garlic, Sesame

Three-Bean Salad

8 portions

**1 portion = approx. 8 grams of usable protein
19% to 23% of average daily protein need**

A tangy and creamy salad. Serve it very cold in a bed of greens.

1/2 cup dry garbanzo
  beans
1/2 cup dry kidney beans
1/2 cup dry black beans
1 cup yogurt
2–4 tbsp lemon juice
1/2 cup milk powder (2/3
  cup instant)
2 tbsp honey

1/2 tsp salt
1/4 tsp curry powder
1 tsp fresh basil or
  1/2 tsp dried
2–3 tbsp chopped fresh
  chives
3 tbsp chopped fresh
  parsley

Cook the beans separately, if possible, to maintain their individual colors. Cook them until tender, but still firm. Drain them well.

Put the yogurt into a small mixing bowl. Stir it with a whisk until it is creamy-smooth. Mix the lemon juice and milk powder to form a smooth paste; whisk the paste into the yogurt. Blend in the honey and herbs.

Pour the dressing over the beans. Toss gently, cover, and refrigerate several hours or overnight before serving.

Pineapple–Corn Muffins

about 15 muffins

1 muffin = approx. 4 grams of usable protein
9% to 11% of average daily protein need

1 cup whole wheat flour
1/3 cup soy flour
3 tsp baking powder
1 tsp salt
1 cup yellow cornmeal
8½ tbsp instant nonfat
   dry milk (about ½ cup)*
2 eggs, beaten
1 cup water (or part water
and part liquid from
   pineapple)
¼ cup melted butter
2 tbsp honey
8 ounces crushed pine-
   apple (unsweetened),
   drained
pineapple preserves (or
   orange marmalade)

Stir together all the dry ingredients, including the dry milk. Combine all the remaining ingredients (except preserves) and stir into dry ingredients. Don't overmix. Fill oiled muffin wells about ⅔ full and top with ¼ to ½ teaspoon of pineapple preserves. Bake at 400°F for about 20 minutes, or until golden. Since these muffins are not very sweet they can be served with the main course. For a dessert muffin you might wish to add more honey.

*There is enough milk powder here to meet the complementary proportions of the corn–soy combination and still have some left to complement the wheat flour.

4

Minestrone con Crema

Roman Rice and Beans

Fine Fruit Salad

Minestrone con Crema

6 to 8 portions

**1 portion = approx. 10 grams of usable protein
23% to 28% of average daily protein need**

¾ cup dry garbanzo
   beans, cooked until
   almost done

Pesto:
½ cup fresh basil, spinach,
   or parsley leaves (dry
   leaves won't work)
1 clove garlic, minced
1 cup grated Parmesan
   cheese
olive oil as needed

5 kohlrabi or turnips with
   leaves chopped (about
   2 cups) and bulbs diced
1 head cabbage, finely
   chopped or grated
2 cups beet greens or
   spinach, without stems,
   chopped
¼ cup chopped parsley
salt to taste
3 cups milk
sherry to taste (optional)

Make a pesto: Mash together in a mortar, or put in a blender, the fresh basil, garlic, and Parmesan cheese with enough olive oil to make a smooth paste.

Put all the vegetables in a pot with the beans and cooking water from beans—plus just enough water to cover. (Seem like a lot of vegetables? Believe me, it works!) Add the parsley and salt, bring to a boil, then simmer about 1 hour. Add the milk and simmer the soup 15 minutes more. Stir in the pesto and optional sherry and heat 5 minutes more. Serve at once. This soup is truly delicious. (A friend who swears that he dislikes both greens and turnips ate this soup with gusto!)

Roman Rice and Beans

8 to 10 portions

1 portion = approx. 11 grams of usable protein
26% to 31% of average daily protein need

oil as needed
2 large onions, finely chopped
2 cloves garlic, crushed
1-2 carrots, finely chopped
1 stalk celery, chopped (optional)
2/3 cup chopped parsley
5-6 tsp dried basil
1 tsp dried oregano
2 large tomatoes, coarsely chopped

4-5 tsp salt
pepper to taste
1½ cups dried beans such as kidney, black, or pinto, cooked till tender
4 cups raw brown rice, cooked with 4 tsp salt
¼-½ cup butter or margarine
1 cup or more grated cheese (Parmesan or jack)

Sauté onions, garlic, carrots, celery, parsley, basil, and oregano in oil until onion is golden. Add tomatoes, salt, pepper, and cooked beans.

Add butter and cheese to cooked rice. Then add first mixture to the rice. Garnish with more parsley and more grated cheese.

Fine Fruit Salad

8 portions

**1 portion = approx. 5 grams of usable protein
12% to 14% of average daily protein need**

3/4 cup roasted peanuts
1 cup raw or roasted
   sunflower seeds
1 cup sliced apples
1 cup sliced bananas
1/2 cup tangerine or
   orange sections
1 cup fresh sliced peaches

1 cup seedless grapes
1/2 cup raisins
1/2 cup shredded coconut
2–4 tbsp honey
juice of 1/2 lemon
1/2 cup wine
10–15 leaves fresh mint

Combine all ingredients in a large bowl and mix thoroughly. Garnish with mint leaves. At different times of the year you can substitute any fruit in season. Just be sure to include the peanuts and sunflower seeds for complementarity.

Other delicious salad ideas using peanuts and sunflower seeds:

Peanut–Sunflower–Carrot Salad: Just combine grated carrots, raisins, peanuts, sunflower seeds, and crushed pineapple (optional) with a dressing of one part peanut butter to two parts mayonnaise.

Peanut–Sunflower Waldorf Salad: Sprinkle lemon juice over diced apples (or pineapple chunks) and celery. Add chopped peanuts and sunflower seeds. Moisten with a dressing of blended mayonnaise and peanut butter.

5

Mediterranean Lemon Soup

Middle Eastern Tacos

Peanut Bars

Mediterranean Lemon Soup

6 portions

1 portion = 6 grams of usable protein
14% to 17% of average daily protein need

1½ quarts of vegetable
   stock (saved from
   cooking vegetables or
   beans)
½ cup raw brown rice
salt, if necessary
¼ tsp summer savory

2 tbsp brewer's yeast
4 eggs, beaten
juice and grated rind of
   1–2 lemons (you can
   start with the smaller
   amount and add more
   to taste at the end)

Heat stock to boiling and stir in rice and salt. Cover and simmer about 30 minutes. Mix savory and yeast into eggs. Add lemon juice and rind and mix again. Take 1 cup of hot stock and slowly add it to the egg mixture, stirring constantly so that eggs don't curdle. Remove stock from heat and gradually add egg mixture to it. Serve.

The clean, fresh taste of this soup makes a perfect beginning to many different types of meals. For instance, it is delicious with the Middle Eastern Tacos, with fish entrées, and with many vegetable casseroles.

Middle Eastern Tacos

10 tacos

2 tacos = approx. 10 grams of usable protein
23% to 28% of average daily protein need

1 cup dry garbanzo beans, cooked	¾ tsp ground coriander
½ cup sesame seeds, toasted, or ¼ cup sesame butter	½ tsp salt
	½ tsp ground cumin
	¼–½ tsp cayenne
2 cloves garlic	10 pieces Middle Eastern
2 tbsp lemon juice	flat bread or 10 wheat tortillas

Purée together ingredients through cayenne (increase
spices to taste). Let stand at least ½ hour at room
temperature. Cut pieces of Middle Eastern flat bread
in half and fill "pockets" with bean mixture; or serve
on wheat tortillas that have been fried until soft (not
crisp). Add the following garnishes and allow everyone
at the table to assemble their own "taco."

shredded lettuce	chopped onion
chopped tomatoes	1½ cups yogurt (or cheese)
chopped cucumber	

Wonderfully tasty and satisfying! Be sure to include
yogurt or cheese on each portion to complete the protein complementarity.

Peanut Bars

36 bars

2 bars = approx. 7 grams of usable protein
15% to 18% of average daily protein need

½ cup peanut butter
½ cup butter
1 cup honey
2 eggs
2 tsp vanilla
1 cup chopped peanuts, roasted or raw
2 cups whole wheat flour

¼ heaping cup milk powder (1/3 heaping cup instant)
1 tsp salt
2 tsp baking powder
½ cup milk (or ½ cup water plus 2 more tbsp milk powder)

Use a large mixing bowl. Cream together the peanut butter and butter. When the mixture is light, cream in the honey. Beat in the eggs one at a time, then beat in the vanilla.

Stir together the peanuts, whole wheat flour, milk powder, salt, and baking powder; add this mixture alternately with the ½ cup milk to the creamed mixture.

Turn the mixture into two 9x9-inch oiled pans (or into pans of equivalent size).

Bake at 350°F for 25 minutes. Cool and cut into bars.

6

Walnut–Cheddar Loaf

Cumin–Cucumber Salad

Bread Pudding
with Lemon Sauce

Walnut–Cheddar Loaf

4 portions

**1 portion = approx. 13 grams of usable protein
30% to 36% of average daily protein need**

1 cup ground black walnuts (can use blender)	2 cups chopped onions, sautéed
1 cup grated cheese	2 eggs, beaten
1/2 cup raw brown rice, cooked	1/4 tsp salt
	2 tbsp nutritional yeast
	1 tsp caraway seeds

Combine all ingredients. Place in oiled loaf pan. Bake at 350°F for 30 minutes.

This loaf is especially nice if served with whole walnuts sprinkled on top and accompanied by a cheese sauce.

Cumin–Cucumber Salad

4 portions

**1 portion = approx. 5 grams of usable protein
11% to 13% of average daily protein need**

Far more interesting than the usual cucumber, sour cream, and parsley mixture, this spicy salad was inspired by a recipe from India.

1 medium-sized cucumber	1 tsp cumin seeds
1 small onion, diced (1/4–1/3 cup)	1/2 cup cottage cheese
1–1 1/2 tsp salt	1/2 cup yogurt
1 tomato, diced	a few sprigs of parsley, chopped

Quarter the cucumber lengthwise, then hold the quarters together and slice them into half-inch chunks. Place in a small bowl.

Add the onion, salt, and tomato to the bowl with the cucumber and toss gently.

Toast the cumin seeds in a small dry frying pan over medium heat only until they are brittle, not browned. It should take about 1 minute.

Place the cottage cheese and yogurt in your blender, add the toasted cumin, and buzz until the mixture is smooth.

Pour the dressing over the salad vegetables, toss gently, and refrigerate for an hour, if possible, before serving.

Bread Pudding with Lemon Sauce

8 portions

1 portion = approx. 8 grams of usable protein
18% to 22% of average daily protein need

Make this pudding with whole wheat bread or whole protein bread that has dried out a little.

4 cups hot milk
2 cups dry whole wheat
  bread cubes
1/2–2/3 cup honey
1 tbsp butter

1 tsp vanilla
1/2 tsp salt
1/2 cup raisins (optional)
4 eggs, slightly beaten

Pour the hot milk over the bread cubes; while they soak, stir in the honey, butter, vanilla, and salt, and optional raisins.

When the mixture has cooled slightly, beat in the eggs.

Pour into an oiled 1½-quart baking dish. Place in a

pan of hot water and bake at 350°F for about 1 hour, until firm.

Serve warm with lemon sauce:

1 tbsp cornstarch	1/4–1/3 cup honey
dash salt	1 1/2 tbsp lemon juice
dash nutmeg	2 tbsp butter
1 cup boiling water	

Combine the cornstarch, salt, and nutmeg in a small saucepan; stir in the hot water gradually and cook over low heat until thick and clear.

Blend in the honey, lemon juice, and butter.

7

Ricotta Lasagne Swirls

Caesar Salad

Chameleon Spice Cake

Ricotta Lasagne Swirls

4 portions

**1 portion = approx. 14 grams of usable protein
32% to 39% of average daily protein need**

8 cooked lasagne noodles

Filling:
2 bunches spinach, finely
   chopped
2 tbsp Parmesan cheese
1 cup ricotta cheese
   (½ pound)
¼ tsp nutmeg
salt and pepper to taste

Sauce:*
2 cups tomato sauce
2 cloves garlic, minced
   and sautéed
½ cup onions, chopped
   and sautéed
½ tsp basil
salt and pepper to taste

Steam spinach until it is quite limp, but not mushy.
You don't need any water to do this. Just put the
washed spinach in a pan with a tight-fitting lid and cook
it over low heat about 7 minutes. Mix the spinach with
the cheeses, nutmeg, salt, and pepper. Coat each noodle
with 2 to 3 tablespoons of the mixture along its entire
length, roll up, turn on end so that you see the spiral,
and place in a shallow baking pan. Mix all of the sauce
ingredients together and pour over all rolled-up noodles.
Bake at 350°F for 20 minutes.

This is an especially attractive dish and much lighter
than most Italian-style pasta dishes.

Variation: Use part of the spinach in the filling and
part in the sauce.

*Or use your favorite Marinara or Spaghetti Sauce.

Chameleon Spice Cake

12 portions

1 portion with frosting = approx. 7 grams of usable protein
16% to 20% of average daily protein need

½ cup soft butter
¾ cup honey
2/3 cup brown sugar
2 eggs
2 cups whole wheat flour
½ cup soy flour
1 tsp ground cinnamon
½ tsp ground nutmeg
½ tsp ground allspice
1 tsp baking soda
1 tsp salt
2 tsp vanilla extract

2/3 cup buttermilk or yogurt

Options:
1) ½ cup carob powder plus 1 tsp instant coffee mixed with 1/3 cup hot water, or
2) 1½ cups mashed bananas, or
3) 4 sliced apples
2/3 cup sunflower seeds or chopped nuts*

Cream the butter, honey, and sugar together. Add eggs and beat until the mixture is fluffy, using electric mixer. Stir all dry ingredients together and add alternately with the vanilla and buttermilk or yogurt—beating continually with the electric mixer. Blend in option 1 or fold in by hand option 2 or 3. Stir in the nuts. Bake at 350°F in two greased 8-inch pans or one long greased pan. Cooking time will vary from 25 to 40 minutes. Cake is done when toothpick comes out "clean." (To avoid sogginess, banana spice bars should be cut into bars while still warm and cooled on a wire rack.)

*Using sunflower seeds and chopped peanuts, you can create another complementary protein combination.

Frosting:
Cream together:
2 tbsp soft butter
1/4 cup honey
1 tsp vanilla

For carob frosting
beat in:
2–3 tbsp milk or
   buttermilk
1/4 cup carob powder

2/3 cup instant powdered
   milk

For spice frosting beat in:
2–3 tbsp milk or
   buttermilk
1 cup instant powdered
   milk
dashes of cinnamon,
   nutmeg, and allspice to
   taste

Whip until smooth, adding more liquid or more powder to create desired consistency. For a fruit frosting, try substituting fruit juice for milk and adding grated orange rind instead of spices. If your child sneaks a fingerful of this frosting off the cake, you don't have to worry. It's good for him.

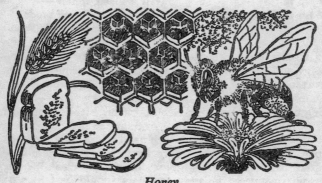

Honey

8

Fruit and Vegetable Salad

Sweet and Pungent Vegetable Curry

Cottage Cheese Cake

Fruit and Vegetable Salad

For a delicious appetizer, combine chunks of apple, carrot, pineapple, celery, and mandarin oranges with a little yogurt and a pinch of grated orange peel.

Sweet and Pungent Vegetable Curry

8 portions

**1 portion = approx. 15 grams of usable protein
35% to 42% of average daily protein need**

2–3 onions, sliced thinly
5 carrots, sliced thickly
vegetable oil as needed
1-1/3 cup soybeans, cooked with about 2 cups extra water
2 cups raw brown rice and 1½ cups raw bulgur, cooked
    together
¼ cup flour
1 tbsp (or more) hot curry powder
1 cup (or more) raisins
1 cup raw cashews
3 tbsp (or more) mango chutney
1 tbsp raw sugar

Sauté onions and carrots in small amount of oil. Add curry powder and flour; cook 1 minute. Stir in liquid from beans (at least 1 cup). Simmer until carrots are tender but not soft. Add remaining ingredients and more liquid if necessary. Adjust seasoning. Simmer until raisins are soft and seasonings mingle. Serve on the grains. A delightful combination—perfect for the most festive occasion.

Curry is a rich dish. Traditionally it is served with many additional side dishes. Try small bowls of yogurt, lightly sprinkled with dill, or finger food of raw, crisp vegetables such as celery, carrots, broccoli. Or skip the fresh fruit appetizer and serve a brisk, tangy salad such as the following:

Slice one medium tomato per person.
Chop fine one medium onion to every three tomatoes.
Stir together 1 tablespoon honey to 3 of vinegar, pour over tomatoes and onions and mix. Add salt to taste.

Corn, Apple, Raisins, Soy

Cottage Cheese Cake

a 10-inch pie of 8 portions

**1 portion = approx. 12 grams of usable protein
29% to 34% of average daily protein need**

A rich cheesecake, but not as rich as those made with sour cream and cream cheese. A lot of protein for dessert!

partially baked pie crust

Cake:
4 eggs
2 cups cottage cheese
1/2 cup honey
1/2 tsp salt
1 tsp lemon juice
    or 1/2 tsp vanilla

cinnamon

Topping:
1 1/2 cups yogurt
2 tbsp honey
1/2 tsp vanilla

Prepare a whole wheat pie crust* (or make your favorite graham cracker or cookie crumb crust), or granola crust (see *Recipes for a Small Planet*, p. 293).

Put the eggs into your blender and buzz until they're whipped; add the cottage cheese 1/2 cup at a time and blend until smooth.

Pour the mixture into a small bowl; stir in the honey, salt, and lemon juice or vanilla.

Turn it into the pie crust, which has been partially baked. Dust with cinnamon and bake at 350°F for about 20 minutes.

Stir together the topping ingredients, pour the mixture over the partially baked pie, and bake another 10 to 15 minutes.

When it is done, a knife inserted in the center will come out clean. Cool the pie on a rack for an hour; then chill several hours or overnight before serving.

*See recipe on page 135.

9

Rice con Queso

Green Beans or Peas, Steamed

Peanut Purée Soufflé

Rice con Queso

6 portions

**1 portion = approx. 17 grams of usable protein
39% to 47% of average daily protein need**

1½ cups raw brown rice,
  cooked with salt and
  pepper
½ cup dry black beans
  (or blackeyed peas),
  cooked
3 cloves garlic, minced or
  crushed
1 large onion, chopped

1 small can chilies,
  chopped
¾ pound shredded jack
  cheese
½ pound ricotta cheese
  thinned slightly with
  milk or yogurt
½ cup grated cheddar
  cheese

Mix rice, beans, garlic, onion, chilies. Layer this mixture alternately in a greased casserole with jack cheese and ricotta (spreading evenly over casserole). End with rice mixture. Bake at 350°F for ½ hour. During last few minutes of baking, sprinkle grated cheddar cheese over the top.

This is an ideal dish for a buffet dinner. My guests always ask for this recipe!

Peanut Purée Soufflé

6 portions

**1 portion = approx. 13 grams of usable protein
29% to 35% of average daily protein need**

A new experience in taste from the flavor of cooked peanuts makes this soufflé truly exotic, and extremely delicious for dessert.

1 cup raw peanuts, cooked
and puréed with 1 cup
of their cooking water—
about 1¾ cups purée
¼ cup milk powder
(1/3 cup instant)
¼ cup honey

1 tsp vanilla
a pinch of salt
5 egg whites or 4 extra
large egg whites, at
room temperature
¼ tsp cream of tartar

Cook the peanuts until they are very tender. To make
a smooth purée easily: buzz the milk powder in a
blender with the 1 cup of the peanut cooking water;
add the peanuts, and buzz again until smooth.

Pour the purée into a small bowl; stir in the honey,
vanilla, and salt. Be sure the purée is at room temperature before going to the next steps.

Put the egg whites in a deep bowl; using a clean wire
whisk or an electric mixer, beat them until they are stiff,
but not dry. Beat in the cream of tartar.

Fold the egg whites into the purée: stir a small blob
of whites into the purée first to lighten it; then fold in the
remaining whites completely, but don't fold more than
you need to make the mixture homogeneous.

Pour the mixture into a buttered 1½- to 2-quart
soufflé dish or deep casserole with straight sides.

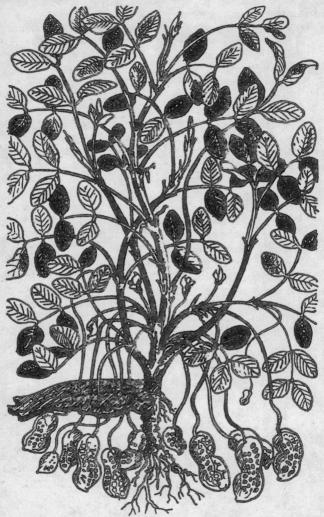

Peanuts grow underground

10

Cashew and Carrot Soup

Potato Kugel

Date and Orange Loaf

Cashew and Carrot Soup

about 2½ quarts

1 cup = approx. 4 grams of usable protein
9% to 11% of average daily protein need

You can serve this soup either hot or cold. Its sweetness comes naturally from the carrots, apples, raisins, cashews, and tomato paste.

1 tbsp butter
¼ cup oil
1½ cups chopped onions
4 cups grated carrots (packed tight for measuring)
3 ounces tomato paste
1 cup chopped apples
6 cups stock
2 tsp salt
1/3 cup raw brown rice
1 cup raisins
1 cup raw chopped cashews
1–3 tsp honey (optional)
2½ cups dairy products (see the last step)

Melt the butter and oil in a soup pot or pressure cooker; sauté the chopped onions for 1 minute, stir in the carrots, and sauté until the onions are soft and transparent. They will be orange rather than brown!

Stir in the tomato paste, apples, stock, and salt. Bring the mixture to a boil and stir in the brown rice.

Cover and pressure cook for 15 minutes, OR cook regularly for about 45 minutes, until the soup is a beautiful orange and the carrots are tender, but not mushy.

(Optional step—remove one cup of soup from the pot; put it in the blender and buzz until smooth; return it to the pot.)

Add the raisins and cashews and optional honey, bring to a boil again, and simmer until the raisins are plump—about 5 minutes.

You may now EITHER: add 2½ cups of milk and

heat through; OR: serve as is but add ¼ cup yogurt to each bowl of soup; OR: serve the soup cold, adding ¼ cup yogurt or buttermilk; OR: serve the soup cold after the 2½ cups of milk have been added.

Cashew nuts

Potato Kugel

a 7x11-inch or 9x9-inch pan;
about 15 squares

2 squares = approx. 9 grams of usable protein
20% to 24% of average daily protein need

The kugel is delicious hot or cold. Decide before baking which topping you prefer, for when cold it can be easily eaten with your hands and it will have better protein if all the cheese is already there.

6 average potatoes
2–3 carrots
1 big onion
1 clove garlic, minced
2 eggs, beaten
3 tbsp oil
2 tsp salt

1/4 cup whole grain bread crumbs
3/4 cup milk powder (1 cup instant)

Topping:
1 cup grated cheese or 2 cups yogurt and 1/3 cup grated cheese

Grate the potatoes, carrots, and the onion into a large bowl (or, to save time, you could cut the carrots and onions into chunks and blend in blender until finely chopped, then add to the grated potatoes). Drain off the liquid that will accumulate around the edges of the mixture before going on.

Stir in all the remaining ingredients, adding the milk powder very carefully to avoid lumps.

Spread the mixture evenly in an oiled pan. Place it in a 350°F oven for 40 minutes to 1 hour. (The square pan will take longer than the 7x11-inch one.) When the kugel is nearly done it will test dry like a cake, the edges should be brown, and it will smell delicious. Before you remove it from the oven, add the grated cheese, either ⅓ or 1 cup. Leave it for about 5 more minutes, or until the cheese is completely melted.

If you are using the smaller amount of cheese, serve the yogurt at the table, using about 2 tablespoons per square. It is just as delicious with the full cup of grated cheese *and* yogurt. If you use the full cup of cheese, you can eat it cold without the yogurt and still get the full amount of protein.

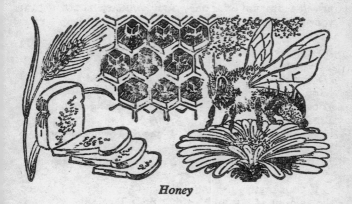

Honey

Date and Orange Loaf

1 loaf of 15 pieces

1 piece = approx. 4 grams of usable protein
9% to 10% of average daily protein need

If you use pitted, very sweet dates such as Deglet Noir, your loaf will be very rich, like a fruit cake. Adjust the amount of honey that you use according to your sweet tooth and your dates.

1/3 cup fresh orange juice
(reserve rind)
2/3 cup hot milk
1 cup chopped dates
1/4 cup soy grits
2 tbsp oil
1/2–3/4 cup honey
2 eggs, beaten
1 tsp vanilla extract

1/4 tsp orange extract
(optional)
2 cups whole wheat flour
1 tsp baking powder
1/2 tsp baking soda
1/2 tsp salt
the rind of one orange,
grated
3/4 cup chopped walnuts

If your orange has more than 1/3 cup of juice, reduce the amount of hot milk so that the total liquid is 1 cup.

Pour the hot mixture over the dates and soy grits; let the mixture soak while you prepare the batter.

Cream the oil and honey; beat in the eggs, vanilla, and optional orange extract.

Stir the dry ingredients together (except the walnuts) and add them alternately with the soaked date mixture to the creamed honey.

Stir in the orange rind and walnuts.

Turn into an oiled loaf pan (5x9 inches); bake at 325°F for 1 hour for a moist bread, 1½ hours for a drier loaf.

11

Feijoada Brazilian Dinner

Tossed Green Salad
with Green Goddess Dressing

Nutty Applesauce Cake

Feijoada Brazilian Dinner
(Tangy Black Beans, Rice with Sauce, Steamed Greens)

6 portions

**1 portion = approx. 11 grams of usable protein
26% to 31% of average daily protein need**

Beans:

1 large onion, chopped
2 cloves garlic, chopped
oil
1 cup dry black beans
3 cups stock or water (or substitute wine for up to half of stock)
1 bay leaf
1/4 tsp pepper
1 orange, whole or halved
1/2 tsp salt
2 stalks celery, chopped
1 tomato, chopped

Sauté the onion and garlic in a little oil, then add them to the beans, with stock, the bay leaf, and pepper. Bring to a boil, simmer 2 minutes, and let sit, covered, for 1 hour. Add the whole or halved orange (whole is the traditional way), salt, celery, and tomato. Simmer, covered, with lid ajar, for 2 to 3 hours or more, until the beans are tender. Remove a ladleful of beans, mash them, and return them to the pot to cook until the mashed beans thicken the mixture.

Rice:

1 onion, chopped
3 cloves garlic, minced
2 tbsp olive oil
2 tbsp butter
2 tomatoes, peeled, seeded, coarsely chopped
2 cups raw brown rice, cooked

Sauté the onion and garlic in the olive oil and butter until the onion is golden. Add the tomatoes, and simmer a few minutes. Stir in the cooked rice and keep warm over low heat.

Sauces for rice:

1 cup lemon juice
1 small onion
2 cloves garlic
1 tomato, peeled and seeded

1 tsp green salsa jalapeña
or 2 ounces canned
California green chilies,
seeded

Blend all ingredients in blender until smooth.

OR

1 tomato, peeled and seeded
California green chilies, seeded, to taste
1 tsp salt

2 cloves garlic
juice of 1 lemon
1 onion, chopped
scallions, parsley, to taste
1/4 cup vinegar

Blend in a blender the first four ingredients until smooth. Stir in the remaining ingredients and, just before serving, stir in a little liquid from the bean pot.

Greens:

1 1/2 pounds trimmed greens
  (turnip or mustard greens, collards, etc.)
1 clove garlic, minced
1 orange, peeled and sliced
6 heaping tbsp toasted sesame seed meal*

Steam first three ingredients together until greens are barely wilted. Sprinkle 1 heaping tablespoon of toasted seed meal on each serving, with orange slices on top.

*Admittedly, sesame seeds are not authentically Brazilian! They are necessary here to complement the "extra" bean protein because this recipe uses more beans than the complementary bean–rice proportions specify. See page 134 for method of toasting.

Here you have a complete Brazilian dinner. Serve the rice with one of the sauces along with the beans and greens to make a splendid three-course meal.

Green Goddess Dressing

about 1 cup

1 cup = approx. 7 grams of usable protein
¼ cup = 4% to 5% of average daily protein need

A cool dressing for summer salads—not too rich.

1 tsp vinegar	2 sprigs fresh parsley
1 large clove garlic	1 tsp dried tarragon
4 whole green onions or 10 large fresh chives	3 tbsp mayonnaise
	1 cup buttermilk

Blend all ingredients (except ¾ cup of the buttermilk) in a blender until smooth.

Stir in the remaining buttermilk. This makes the dressing somewhat thicker than if all the buttermilk is blended.

Nutty Applesauce Cake

sixteen 2-inch squares

1 square = approx. 3 grams of usable protein
7% to 8% of average daily protein need

1 cup applesauce	1 tsp baking soda
¾ cup honey	½ tsp each salt, cinnamon, ginger, cloves
1/3 cup oil or melted butter	
1¼ cups whole wheat flour	1/3–2/3 cup roasted peanuts, ground*
1/3 cup soy flour	½–1 cup sunflower seeds*

Mix together the applesauce, honey, and oil. Stir together the remaining ingredients and blend into the liquid. Bake in an 8-inch-square pan for 30 minutes at 350°F. The pan should be oiled and floured.

*The larger amount of nuts and seeds makes a very nutty cake, but will increase the amount of protein.

Sunflower and seeds

Rice

12

Confetti Rice

Garbanzo–Cheese Salad

Gingerbread

Confetti Rice

4 portions

**1 portion = approx. 7 grams of usable protein
16% to 20% of average daily protein need**

oil as needed
1 small onion, chopped
1 cup mixed dried fruits,
 chopped
2/3 cup mixed nuts,*
 chopped

1/3 cup sesame seeds or
 1/2 cup seed meal
1/4–1/2 tsp cloves
1/2 tsp salt
1 cup raw brown rice,
 cooked
4 tbsp melted butter

In hot oil, sauté onion, mixed fruits, nuts, and sesame seed or meal until the onion is golden. Stir in the cloves and salt, and then mix with the cooked rice. Place in a small casserole. Pour the melted butter over all. Bake 15 to 20 minutes at 350°F.

*If you use peanuts and add sunflower seeds to complement their protein, you will probably have lots more usable protein.

Rice and Legumes

Garbanzo–Cheese Salad

4 to 5 portions

**1 portion = approx. 8 grams of usable protein
19% to 22% of average daily protein need**

½ cup dry garbanzo
   beans, cooked and
   cooled
½ bunch red leaf lettuce,
   torn up
½ bunch spinach, torn
½ cup sliced scallions
1 green pepper, chopped
½ cup fresh peas

½ cup raw yellow
   crookneck squash, diced
   or sliced
½ cup cucumber,
   chopped or sliced
1 cup bean or alfalfa
   sprouts
2/3 cup grated cheese

Combine all ingredients, sprinkle with favorite dressing, and serve on a bed of greens.

Naturally, you can use any combination of fresh vegetables that are available; just be sure to include the garbanzo beans and cheese.

Gingerbread

a 9x9-inch pan of 12 pieces

**1 piece = approx. 4 grams of usable protein
9% to 10% of average daily protein need**

A dark molasses gingerbread—delicious with yogurt and fruit.

1¾ cups whole wheat flour
½ cup soy flour, scant
½ tsp salt
1 tsp baking soda
2 tsp baking powder

1 tbsp freshly grated ginger root
2 eggs, beaten
1/3 cup oil or melted butter
1 cup unsulfured molasses
¾ cup hot water

Stir the dry ingredients together (include the fresh ginger root here too).

Stir the remaining liquid ingredients together. They won't blend very well, but you just want them to be together.

Add the liquid to the dry mixture and blend with a few swift strokes. Immediately place the mixture in a well-oiled baking pan.

Bake at 325°F for 30 to 35 minutes, until the cake tests done.

13

Bulgur and Garbanzos

Green Salad
with Herbed Cottage Cheese Dressing

Spiced Pear Muffins

Bulgur and Garbanzos

6 portions

**1 portion = approx. 8 grams of usable protein
17% to 21% of average daily protein need**

This quick dish goes beautifully with steamed summer squash and butter. Quick bread or muffins and a salad round out the meal.

1¼ cups raw bulgur wheat	1 tbsp tamari soy sauce
3 tbsp oil	¾ cup garbanzo beans,
2½ cups stock	cooked tender
1 bay leaf (remove before	oil
serving)	1 cup yogurt
1 tsp dill seeds	

Sauté the bulgur in the oil for about 5 minutes until it sizzles and is slightly brown. Add more oil if it sticks to the pan.

Add the stock, bay leaf, dill seeds, and soy sauce to the bulgur. Bring to a boil, lower the heat, cover and simmer until all of the stock is absorbed.

While the bulgur is cooking, sauté the garbanzos in an oiled frying pan for about 10 minutes. Add oil as needed. The garbanzos won't get crisp like nuts, but they should brown on the outside.

When the bulgur is cooked, stir in the garbanzos and 1 cup yogurt. Let the mixture stand for a few minutes to allow the grains to absorb the yogurt. Then serve.

Herbed Cottage Cheese Dressing

about 2 cups

2 cups = approx. 37 grams of usable protein
¼ cup = 11% to 13% of average daily
protein need

You can really use any fresh herbs for this dressing.

2/3 cup fresh parsley
1 tbsp fresh rosemary
½ tsp salt
¼ cup oil

¼ cup apple cider
  vinegar
½–1 cup milk
1 cup cottage cheese

Buzz all ingredients in the blender until smooth. The amount of milk you use will determine the thickness of the dressing.

Try substituting any of these fresh herbs: basil, chives, dill, coriander, mint, thyme, oregano, tarragon, or summer savory.

Spiced Pear Muffins

12 muffins

2 muffins = approx. 6 grams of usable protein
15% to 18% of average daily protein need

This spiced muffin is delicious and fruity for breakfast, but not too sweet to accompany your dinner.

1-2/3 cups whole wheat
 flour
1/3 cup soy flour
1 tbsp baking powder
1/2 tsp salt
1/2 tsp cinnamon
1/4 tsp nutmeg
1/2 cup chopped pears
 (about 1/2-inch pieces);
 use fresh or drained,
 canned pears

1 egg, beaten
1 cup milk or 1 cup water
 plus 1/4 cup milk powder
 (1/3 cup instant)
1-4 tbsp melted butter
 or oil
1-4 tbsp honey

Stir the dry ingredients together with the spices in a small bowl; add the chopped pears and distribute them gently throughout the flour mixture.

Blend the liquid ingredients together and then pour them into the dry all at once. Stir 12 times or less to moisten.

Fill oiled muffin tins 2/3 full; bake at 400°F for about 25 minutes, until nicely browned. Serve hot.

14

Sesame Tomatoes on Rice

Green Salad
with Dilled Yogurt Dressing

"Casserolls"

Sesame Tomatoes on Rice

6 portions

**1 portion = approx. 7 grams of usable protein
17% to 20% of average daily protein need**

A colorful dish with the surprise of sesame. Add to it a green salad or steamed green vegetables for a beautiful meal.

1/4 cup sesame oil
1 1/2 cups chopped onions
2 cups raw brown rice
3 1/2 cups water (for pressure cooker) or 4 cups
1 tsp salt
1 tsp dried oregano
2/3 cup sesame seeds, ground (about 1 cup meal)
1–2 tsp salt
2 eggs, beaten
12–15 1/2-inch-thick tomato slices, from firm red or green tomatoes
chunks of fresh tomato
sprigs of fresh oregano
sprigs of fresh parsley

Heat the oil in the bottom of your pressure cooker or in a regular saucepan for cooking rice.

Sauté the chopped onions until they are golden, add the raw rice, and continue to sauté until the whole mixture is golden. Add the 3½ cups water (or 4 cups for regular cooking), salt, and oregano. Stir, cover, and cook until the rice is tender.

While the rice cooks, stir the sesame meal and salt together in a flat dish or pie plate. Oil a large frying pan and turn the heat high.

Dip the tomato slices in the beaten egg, then into the sesame mixture, coating both sides well. Fry the slices quickly in hot oil to brown the coating and heat them through. You don't want the tomatoes to get mushy, so keep the heat high. As soon as they are brown, remove

them from the pan. Any leftover egg can be stir-fried
into the rice. Simply make a hole in the cooked rice so
that the beaten egg can be poured in on the hot bottom
to cook. Scramble with a spatula as it cooks and mix
into the rice.

Arrange the rice on a platter or shallow bowl. Place
the sesame-browned tomatoes over the rice. Top with
fresh tomato chunks, sprigs of oregano and parsley.
Sprinkle with a little soy sauce to taste for a moister
dish. Serve while it's hot.

Dilled Yogurt Dressing

about 2 cups

2 cups = approx. 7 grams of usable protein
¼ cup = 2% of average daily protein need

This sharp dressing will perk up any vegetable dish
or salad.

1 cup yogurt
2 tbsp vinegar
½ small onion
½ tsp salt
½ tsp dill seeds

¼ tsp dry mustard
¼ tsp minced garlic or
  garlic powder
pepper (optional)

Process all the ingredients in a blender until the onion
is completely puréed.

"Casserolls"

a 9x9-inch pan of 12 rolls

2 rolls = approx. 4 grams of usable protein
9% to 10% of average daily protein need

These are rich, buttery, crusty rolls. Serve them hot right out of your casserole dish.

1 cup milk	1 tbsp baking yeast
1 tbsp honey	1½ cups whole wheat
¼ cup butter, divided	flour
½ tsp salt	

Heat the milk, honey, 1 tablespoon of the butter, and the salt until the butter melts and the honey dissolves. Place the mixture in another bowl to cool to about 100°F.

While the mixture cools, melt the remaining butter and then set it aside to cool.

Add the yeast to the milk mixture. Stir to dissolve and then let it sit until it bubbles a little. Add the whole wheat flour; beat the dough 50 strokes, until smooth and elastic.

It won't be dry like a bread dough, but it also does not require kneading. Let the dough rise about 30 minutes.

Pour ½ of the reserved melted butter on the bottom of a 9x9-inch baking pan or casserole. Stir the batter down, then drop it by heaping tablespoons into the buttery pan. Pour the remaining butter over the rolls; let rise until double.

Bake at 400°F for 30 minutes. Serve hot from the pan.

15

Mushroom Curry

Kidney Bean Salad

Cheese-Filled Coffee Cake

Mushroom Curry

8 portions

1 portion = approx. 7 grams of usable protein 15% to 19% of average daily protein need

A delicious one-dish meal, or add a salad for a simple feast.

1/2 pound fresh mushrooms—chop the stems and leave the caps whole
2–3 tbsp butter
1 onion, minced
1 tbsp curry powder
2 apples, chopped fine (chop one of the apples just before serving)

paprika
salt
2-2/3 cups yogurt
2 cups raw brown rice, cooked and hot or 1 1/2 cups bulgur wheat, cooked and hot

Sauté the mushroom caps in butter for about 5 minutes, until they just absorb the butter and get slightly brown. Set them aside in a small bowl.

Add more butter to the pan and sauté the onion and curry powder until the onion is almost transparent. Add 1 chopped apple and the mushroom stems; continue sautéeing until the onion is transparent. Don't let the apple get too mushy. Remove from the heat and stir in paprika, salt to taste, and the yogurt.

To assemble the dish: Place the cooked grain in a 2- or 2½-quart casserole. Spread the mushroom—yogurt sauce evenly over the grain. Then arrange the mushroom caps on the top. Sprinkle with more paprika.

Bake the casserole at 350°F until the sauce is firm. Sprinkle the freshly chopped apple over the top just before serving.

Variation: Instead of a casserole dish, use a shallow 7x11-inch baking dish. Arrange the ingredients as indicated above and bake until the sauce is firm.

Quick Mushroom Curry: Stir the sautéed mushroom caps into the yogurt sauce and either combine the sauce with the cooked grain OR serve the mushrooms and sauce over the cooked grain. Do not bake the curry. You may also stir the uncooked chopped apple in with the caps.

Green pepper, Scallions, Mushrooms, Garlic

Kidney Bean Salad

6 portions

**1 portion = approx. 7 grams of usable protein
17% to 21% of average daily protein need**

Serve this salad on a bed of greens. It's refreshing in the summer and is also a good accompaniment to a hot meal in any season.

1 cup dry kidney beans, cooked and drained
1 green pepper, chopped (about ¾ cup)
½ cup chopped onions or scallions
1 tsp crushed or minced garlic
½ cup olive oil
¼ cup wine vinegar
⅛ tsp paprika
¼ tsp salt
1 tsp honey
1 tsp Worcestershire sauce
1 tbsp catsup
dash hot sauce
2 tbsp chopped fresh parsley
1 cup yogurt whisked with . . .
¼ cup milk powder

Combine the cooked beans, green pepper, onions or scallions, and garlic.

Make a dressing of the olive oil, wine vinegar, and the remaining ingredients *except* the yogurt and milk powder.

Pour the dressing over the bean mixture and toss gently. Refrigerate this marinade at least 1 hour.

Just before serving, stir in the yogurt–milk powder mixture.

Cucumber–Kidney Bean Salad: Add 1 chopped cucumber plus ½ to 1 cup chopped celery to the salad before marinating.

Cheese-Filled Coffee Cake

two 9-inch rings of 10 pieces each

1 piece = approx. 7 grams of usable protein
16% to 20% of average daily protein need

This is a most elegant dessert. Toast the leftovers if there are any. When I make it everyone keeps eating and eating until it's all gone. If you make it in a ring mold or spring-form pan that has a fancy bottom, it's especially attractive, since you turn it over before serving.

I cup melted butter
¾ cup honey
I cup yogurt or buttermilk
5–6 egg yolks, beaten until thick and light-colored
2 tbsp baking yeast dissolved in . . .

½ cup warm water
6-1/3 cups whole wheat flour
1-1/6 cups soy flour

Filling:
I cup ricotta cheese
2 eggs, beaten
I tsp vanilla
½ cup honey

Blend the melted butter, honey, and yogurt into the beaten egg yolks; stir in the dissolved yeast.

Stir together the whole wheat flour and soy flour in a large mixing bowl. Remove about 3 cups of the mixture and set it aside (to add later during the kneading).

Pour the yeast and egg mixture into the large bowl full of flour; blend the ingredients together. It should be wet and soft, but not sticky. Knead for about 5 minutes until the dough is smooth, adding the reserved 3 cups of flour if it *is* sticky.

Put the dough back in the bowl, set in a warm place, and let rise until double.

While the cake is rising, prepare the filling: Put the

ricotta cheese through a sieve or beat it vigorously with an electric mixer until it is smooth; blend in the eggs, vanilla, and honey.

Punch down the dough, knead a few times, and divide it into 2 pieces. Roll each piece into a 13-inch circle. Fit each circle over a ring mold, gently lifting it to rest on the bottom, and letting some of the dough hang over the outside edge. Pour ½ the filling into the well of dough in each pan. Lift the outside edges of the dough, bring them over the filling, and seal them by pinching them to the inside ring. Cut a cross in the dough that covers the center ring, then fold those flaps down over the dough covering the filling. Pinch to seal. The filling should be completely sealed.

Let the cake rise until the dough reaches the top of the pans. Bake the cakes at 350°F for 30 minutes. Test with a toothpick for a completely baked cake.

Cool the rings 10 minutes in the pan, then turn onto racks top-side down. Serve at room temperature (top-side down).

16

Peanut Soup

Moist Cornbread

Easy Cole Slaw

Peanut Soup

1½ quarts

1 cup = 16 grams of usable protein
37% to 45% of average daily protein need

A bowl of this soup for lunch and you have nearly half your daily protein accounted for. Your kids should like the peanutty taste, too.

3 tbsp butter
½ cup chopped onions
½ cup chopped celery
2 tbsp whole wheat flour
1 quart stock
¼ tsp celery seed
½ tsp salt

1 cup smooth peanut butter
2 tsp lemon juice
¾ cup milk
1 cup toasted sunflower seeds

Melt the butter in a soup pot or dutch oven; sauté the onions and celery until they are soft. Stir in the whole wheat flour and cook for about 1 minute. Add the stock, celery seed, and salt.

Bring the mixture to a boil, lower the heat, and simmer about 25 minutes.

To incorporate the peanut butter, EITHER add it to the hot soup ¼ cup at a time while mashing it until it melts, OR use your blender: put about 2 cups of soup in the blender; add the peanut butter a little at a time and blend until smooth. If you have only crunchy peanut butter around, this process will make it smooth.

When the peanut butter has been returned to the pot, add the lemon juice, then the milk, and heat again. (If you like a thinner soup, add more milk and adjust the seasoning.) Serve the soup immediately, sprinkling 2 to 3 tablespoons of the toasted sunflower seeds over each cupful.

Moist Cornbread

a 7x11-inch or 9x9-inch pan;
about 15 pieces

2 pieces = approx. 7 grams of usable protein
15% to 18% of average daily protein need

This cornbread is moist and rich, a perfect accompaniment to soups, salads, or bean dishes. It is most delicious when eaten warm with butter or honey, or both!

1 cup cornmeal	1 egg, beaten
1 cup whole wheat flour	3 cups buttermilk or
3 tbsp soy grits	yogurt
2 tsp baking powder	1/4 cup oil
1/2 tsp baking soda	1/4 cup honey
1/2 tsp salt	

Stir together all of the dry ingredients in a large bowl.
Stir the liquid ingredients together in a separate bowl and then stir them into the dry ingredients, mixing only enough to combine the ingredients thoroughly. Less mixing will make a more tender bread.

Pour the batter into an oiled pan and bake at 350°F for 40 to 50 minutes. The top will spring back when the bread is done, and a tester should come out clean, although it may be somewhat wet—*i.e.,* there shouldn't be any uncooked batter on it, but it may be wetter than you would normally expect.

Easy Cole Slaw Dressing

about 1 cup

1 cup = approx. 24 grams of usable protein
**¼ cup = 14% to 17% of average daily
protein need**

Use this dressing on cabbage or carrot salad. Add some peanuts, sunflower seeds, and raisins for a delicious treat!

1/3 cup yogurt	1 tbsp honey
2/3 cup cottage cheese	1 tsp vinegar

Whip all ingredients in a blender until they're smooth and creamy.

17

Eggplant Elegant

Tossed Green Salad

Stewed Fruit
with Spiced Sesame Bars

Eggplant Elegant

6 portions

**1 portion = approx. 14 grams of usable protein
32% to 39% of average daily protein need**

This dish was delicious and filling with a salad along-side. We put tomato sauce on top of the leftovers and reheated them the next day. They were still delicious!

Sauce:

1 onion, chopped
2 cloves garlic, chopped
1/4 pound mushrooms,
  chopped
oil

1 can tomato paste
2–3 cups canned tomatoes
2–3 tsp oregano
1 tsp basil
1 tsp honey

Sauté the onion, garlic, and mushrooms in a small amount of oil in a 2-quart saucepan.

Stir in the tomato paste and remaining ingredients. Add a little water if necessary.

Simmer the sauce while you prepare the rest of the dish.

Batter:

1 cup whole wheat flour
1/4 tsp salt
4 eggs, beaten
water

Eggplant:

1 medium eggplant
oil
1/2 pound cheese

Stir together the flour and salt. Add the beaten eggs to the flour and mix lightly, adding enough water to make a very thick batter. You want the batter to coat the eggplant without sliding off.

Peel the eggplant and slice it into 1/2-inch rounds.

Dip each slice into the batter, then fry in hot oil until golden.

Arrange the batter-fried slices on a baking sheet.

You may use sliced mozzarella or jack cheese, or grated Parmesan mixed with jack or mozzarella. Put a slice of cheese or grated cheese on each round of eggplant.

Place the baking dish (with the eggplant slices topped with cheese) into a 350°F oven for about 10 minutes, until the cheese is melted and the eggplant is very hot.

Serve at once topped with the tomato sauce.

Spiced Sesame Bars

an 8x8-inch pan of 9 pieces

1 piece = approx. 3 grams of usable protein
7% to 8% of average daily protein need

Soft cake with the crunch of sesame . . .

2 eggs, beaten	½ tsp salt
½ cup honey	¼ tsp baking soda
3 tbsp sesame oil	¼ tsp allspice
½ cup whole wheat flour	¼ tsp mace
1 tbsp soy grits	½ tsp cinnamon
1 tbsp milk powder	¼ cup toasted sesame
(1½ tbsp instant)	seeds

Combine the eggs, honey, and oil.

Stir the dry ingredients together (*except* the sesame seeds), add to the egg mixture, and blend.

Oil an 8x8-inch pan; sprinkle ½ of the sesame seeds on the bottom, pour in the batter, and top with the remaining seeds.

Bake at 350°F for 20 minutes. Cool and cut into bars.

18

Complementary Pie

Salad Collage

Banana Spice Bars

Complementary Pie

8 portions

**1 portion = approx. 8 grams of usable protein
19% to 21% of average daily protein need**

This is a good main course when accompanied by a tossed salad. It's creamy and somewhat rich, but ever-so-hard to stop eating!

¾ cup raw brown rice
  or barley, cooked
½ cup dry beans, cooked
  (use large colorful beans
  like kidneys or black)
2 cups sliced onions
1 tbsp butter
1 cup milk

2 eggs, beaten
1 cup grated cheddar
  cheese
1 tsp salt
1 tsp crushed dried
  tarragon
½ tsp Worcestershire
  sauce

While the rice and beans are cooking, sauté the sliced onions in the butter until they are very soft and just begin to turn golden. Set them aside.

Beat the milk into the eggs; stir in the grated cheese, salt, tarragon, and Worcestershire sauce. Then fold in the sautéed onions, cooked beans, and cooked rice.

Turn the mixture into an oiled 10-inch pie plate.

Bake at 325°F for 25 to 30 minutes, until the custard has set and the edges are browned. Let stand for 10 minutes before serving, then slice into wedges.

Complementary Pie with a Crust: Prepare any whole wheat pie crust for a more elegant pie.* There is plenty of extra cheese to complement the wheat. Use a larger

*See recipe on page 135.

pie pan, press the crust in, pour in the custard, and bake as above.

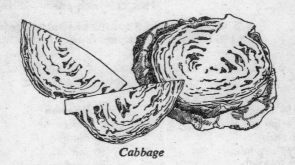

Cabbage

Salad Collage

The protein in this salad depends entirely on you.

shredded cabbage
torn lettuce
raisins
grated fresh coconut
cheese cubes
peanuts and sunflower
   seeds*
leftover cooked but cold

vegetables, including
   potatoes
whole grain croutons†
chopped fresh pineapple

Dressing:
1 part mayonnaise
2 parts yogurt

Mix the dressing in the bottom of a large bowl. Try to judge the amount by the size salad you intend to make.

Add the remaining ingredients and toss to coat them all.

*Be sure to use the peanuts and sunflower seeds in a ratio of 4 to 3.

†To make whole grain croutons: Cut thick slices of whole grain or whole protein bread and then cube the slices. Sauté the cubes in butter until they're crisp and fragrant.

Banana Spice Bars

two 9x9-inch pans—18 bars

1 bar = approx. 5 grams of usable protein
11% to 13% of average daily protein need

These bars are as light as cake, but solidly full of the crunch of sunflower seeds, peanuts, and soy grits.

1½ cups mashed, very ripe bananas	2 tsp cinnamon
2 eggs	1 tsp allspice
2/3 cup honey	½ tsp nutmeg
¼ cup oil	½ tsp salt
½ cup buttermilk or yogurt	¼ tsp cardamom
¼ tsp almond extract	1 tbsp baking powder
2 cups whole wheat flour	1 tsp baking soda
¼ cup soy grits	½ cup chopped peanuts
	2/3 cup sunflower seeds

Put the bananas, eggs, honey, oil, buttermilk, and almond extract into your blender; buzz until smooth.

In a large mixing bowl stir together all the remaining ingredients; make a deep well and pour in the blender mixture. Combine the mixtures completely, but don't overmix.

Pour the batter into two well-oiled pans. Bake at 350°F for 30 to 35 minutes, until the cake is well browned on top, dark around the edges, and pulls away from the sides of the pan.

Cut into bars while the cake is still warm; set the pans on racks to cool.

19

Bean Stroganoff

Tossed Green Salad

Irish Soda Bread

Frozen Cream Cheese and Yogurt Pie

Bean Stroganoff

6 portions

**1 portion = approx. 12 grams of usable protein
28% to 34% of average daily protein need**

The flavor of Stroganoff doesn't really require beef.
Try this recipe and you'll agree.

1/4 cup oil and butter
1 1/2 cups sliced onions
3 cups chopped
  mushrooms
1/4 cup whole wheat flour
3/4 cup stock
1/4 cup sherry
1 1/2–2 tsp salt
2 tsp Worcestershire
  sauce

2 tsp dry mustard
a few grindings fresh
  nutmeg
1 cup dry soybeans,
  cooked
1 1/2 cups yogurt
1 1/2 cups raw bulgur
  wheat, cooked and hot

Heat 2 tablespoons oil and 2 tablespoons butter (or
any combination you prefer) in a large cast-iron frying
pan. Sauté the onions and mushrooms until they are
soft.

Stir in the whole wheat flour and cook for about 2
minutes until the flour has browned lightly and has
coated all of the vegetables.

Stir in the stock, sherry, salt, Worcestershire, mustard,
and nutmeg; cook until the mixture is thick. It will be
very thick until the other ingredients are added.

Stir in the cooked soybeans and cook over low heat
until they are heated through. Remove from the heat
and stir in the yogurt. You should have a luscious
creamy mixture now.

Serve the Stroganoff over the cooked bulgur while
it's hot.

Accompany the Stroganoff with a tossed green salad and the following delicious bread:

Irish Soda Bread

1 small round loaf of 12 slices

1 slice = approx. 3 grams of usable protein
7% to 8% of average daily protein need

This bread is so easy to make, and superb when served hot from the oven with butter. It can also be sliced like yeast bread for sandwiches or toast.

2 cups whole wheat flour
1/2 tsp salt
1 tsp baking soda
1/8 tsp ground cardamom (optional)

1 tbsp honey
1 cup yogurt or buttermilk
1 egg, beaten

Stir the dry ingredients together.

Beat the honey and buttermilk into the beaten egg; gradually pour this mixture into the dry ingredients. The combined mixture will be dry like a yeast bread dough. Blend it with your hands to work all of the flour in. If it is too dry, add a little buttermilk; if too wet, add more whole wheat flour.

Knead the bread for about 5 minutes, then shape into a flat but round loaf.

Place the loaf on an oiled baking sheet; cut two parallel slashes in the dough about 1/2 inch deep. This allows the dough to rise during baking without cracking.

Bake the bread at 375°F for 25 to 30 minutes, until it is well browned and tests done like yeast bread: Tap the bottom, and if it sounds hollow and a toothpick comes out clean, it's done.

Frozen Cream Cheese and Yogurt Pie

a 9-inch pie of 8 portions

**1 portion = approx. 5 grams of usable protein
11% to 14% of average daily protein need**

A luscious pie that's easy to assemble. Keep it frozen
or it will turn to soup. Garnish with any fresh fruit
that's in season.

a 9-inch pie crust made
from 1/2 recipe Whole
Wheat Pie Crust*
1 cup cream cheese,
softened to room
temperature—try to
obtain cream cheese
without additives like
vegetable gum

2/3 cup yogurt
1/4 cup milk powder (1/3
cup instant)
1/2 cup honey
vanilla or almond
flavoring (optional)
fruit in season

Bake the pie crust at 375°F for about 15 minutes.
Cool it while you make the filling.

Beat the cream cheese and yogurt together with a
wire whisk (or electric mixer, if you prefer) until the
mixture is smooth. Whisk in the milk powder 2 tablespoons at a time; then whisk in the honey.

Add a few drops of flavoring if you wish. You might
try lemon or orange, too. Pour the filling into the cooled
pie shell and put it into the freezer.

If you are fond of frozen fruit, you may garnish the
pie before freezing. Otherwise, when the pie is firm,
garnish with fruit and then serve.

*See recipe on page 135.

20

Fesenjon (Spiced Ground Beans)

Cool Slaw

Banana Bread

Fesenjon (Spiced Ground Beans)

8 portions

1 portion = approx. 16 grams of usable protein
38% to 45% of average daily protein need

This is an adaptation of a Persian dish made with ground lamb and walnuts. Its sweet spiciness is unusual and delicious.

1 cup dry soybeans, cooked
1¼ cups raw peanuts, cooked
2 large onions, chopped (about 3 cups)
1 tbsp curry powder
1/3 cup oil
1½ cups catsup
1 cup stock—more if needed
1 tbsp plus 1 tsp salt
2 tsp allspice
2 tbsp cinnamon
1 tsp powdered ginger
1 tsp ground nutmeg
⅞ cup sesame seeds, roasted and ground (see p. 134)
1½ cups raw brown rice, cooked and then mixed with ...
1-1/3 cups raw bulgur, cooked or. 1 cup whole wheat berries, cooked

You may cook the soybeans and peanuts together; then grind them in a food grinder using the small blade, or chop finely all of the cooked beans and peanuts.

In a 4-quart dutch oven sauté the onions and curry powder in the oil until the onions are very soft. Stir in the catsup, stock, salt, and spices.

Add the ground beans-and-peanut mixture and more stock if it is needed. The mixture should have the consistency of (excuse me) a meat sauce you might make for spaghetti. Cover the mixture and simmer it at least 15 minutes, adding stock if necessary.

Stir in the sesame meal, and the fesenjon is ready

to serve over the rice and wheat. Include a salad and yellow vegetable for a delicious meal.

Cool Slaw

4 portions

**1 portion = approx. 12 grams of usable protein
29% to 34% of average daily protein need**

This is an unusual banana-flavored dressing you should like . . .

1 cup grated carrots
2 cups shredded cabbage
½ cup peanuts, raw or
  roasted

2/3 cup sunflower seeds,
  raw or roasted
½ cup raisins
½ cup diced apple

Toss all the ingredients together with this dressing:

½ banana
1/3 cup buttermilk

½ cup ricotta cheese
¼ cup apple juice

Process the dressing in a blender until it's very smooth. Its creaminess is a delightful contrast to the textures of the vegetables, nuts, and seeds.

Banana Bread

a 5x9-inch loaf of 12 slices

1 slice = approx. 4 grams of usable protein
9% to 11% of average daily protein need

This is a rich loaf, and delicious served warm. Cut it carefully and spread with ricotta or cream cheese. And if there's any left over, toast it for breakfast.

1/4 cup butter
2/3 cup honey
3 eggs, beaten
1 cup mashed banana
  pulp (from about 3
  small bananas)
1/3 cup water
1 tsp vanilla

1/4 cup milk powder (1/3
  cup instant)
1 tsp salt
2 tsp baking powder
1 tsp baking soda
2 cups whole wheat flour
walnuts and raisins
  (optional)

Cream the butter and honey (with an electric mixer, if possible) until light; beat in the eggs, banana pulp, water, and vanilla.

Stir together the dry ingredients; stir them into the first mixture, blending with as few strokes as possible.

Stir in 1 cup walnuts and ½ to 1 cup raisins, if desired.

Turn the batter into an oiled loaf pan; bake at 325°F for about 1 hour, until well browned and a toothpick comes out clean.

21

Curried Garbanzo Soup

Wheatless Flat Bread

Crusted Cauliflower

Curried Garbanzo Soup

4 portions

**1 portion = approx. 6 grams of usable protein
13% to 15% of average daily protein need**

This soup is a fine example of how a rich stock can make a simple soup flavorful and unusual. If you have a mild stock, you may want to add other seasonings. Carrots and celery add a touch of sweetness to a pungent base.

4 cups stock
½ cup dry garbanzo
    beans cooked tender
    (see p. 132)
1 tsp curry powder

¼ cup milk powder (1/3
    cup instant)
1 stalk celery, chopped
1 large carrot, sliced
    small
salt and pepper to taste

Heat the stock, then remove a small amount of it for puréeing the garbanzos. Buzz the beans in a blender, then add them to the stock pot.

Sprinkle in the curry, and add the milk powder. (You might blend the milk powder in the blender as long as it's already been used.)

Bring the soup to a boil; add the celery, carrots, and salt and pepper. Simmer the soup until the vegetables are tender but not mushy. Serve hot, or try it cold if there is some left over.

A hot bread goes perfectly with soup, followed by a crusty, delicate vegetable soufflé.

Wheatless Flat Bread

12 pieces

1 piece = approx. 3 grams of usable protein
7% to 8% of average daily protein need

The first time I made this bread I couldn't believe that I had really made it with rye flour: It was so tender and sweet. Do serve it hot with cream cheese, ricotta, or butter.

2 cups rye flour
½ tsp salt
2 tsp baking powder
1 tbsp honey

1 cup double milk*
2 tbsp melted butter
  or oil

Combine the dry ingredients, including any milk powder that you might be using for double milk, if you haven't already mixed it.

Stir the liquid ingredients together, then stir them into the dry mixture until a smooth dough forms.

Oil and flour a cookie sheet or large baking pan (I use a cast-iron frying pan). Place the dough in the pan, flour your hands, and pat it into a large circle (or square) that is ½ inch thick.

Prick the dough with a fork many times and bake it at 450°F until lightly browned—about 10 minutes.

*Double milk is a term I invented for milk that has the protein content of 2 cups of milk and 1 cup of water. To make 1 cup of it, add ½ cup milk powder (⅔ cup instant) to 1 cup water OR mix 1 cup milk and ¼ cup milk powder (⅓ cup instant). A cup of canned evaporated milk would also be equivalent in protein.

Crusted Cauliflower

6 portions

**1 portion = approx. 9 grams of usable protein
21% to 25% of average daily protein need**

Although this casserole contains no eggs, it has a
soufflé-like texture. The grain and cheese crust gives an
interesting contrast to the smoothness of the cauliflower.
You will find this to be an unusual and delightful way
to eat cauliflower.

3 cups steamed
  cauliflower
½ cup stock
½ cup grated cheese
½ cup chopped peanuts,
  raw or roasted
3 tbsp brewer's yeast
¼ cup soy flour

½ cup wheat germ
¼ tsp ground nutmeg
½ cup raw brown rice
  (or whole wheat
  or whole oats), cooked
grated cheese
nutmeg

Buzz the cauliflower and ½ cup stock in the blender
until it's very smooth. You should have about 2 cups of
purée.

Stir the grated cheese, peanuts, brewer's yeast, soy
flour, wheat germ, and nutmeg into the purée; turn the
mixture into an oiled 2-quart casserole.

Fluff the cooked grain with a fork; carefully sprinkle
it over the purée. Top with more grated cheese and
another dash of nutmeg.

Bake the casserole at 350°F for 20 to 25 minutes.

22

Corn and Bean Chowder

Noodle Surprise

Green Salad
with Easy Yogurt Dressing

Corn and Bean Chowder

about 1½ quarts

1 cup = approx. 6 grams of usable protein
15% to 18% of average daily protein need

This is not a thick chowder, but it's still hearty.

¼ cup oil	6 tbsp milk powder
2 cups sliced onions	(½ cup instant)
2 tsp minced garlic	½ cup dry black or
4 cups corn, either	kidney beans, cooked
fresh or frozen	just tender, and drained
4 cups stock	½ tsp salt
¼ tsp nutmeg	

Heat the oil in a large soup pot or cast-iron dutch oven. Stir in the onions and garlic; sauté them until the onions are very soft, but not browned.

Add 3 cups of the corn, the stock, and nutmeg; bring the mixture to a boil, then simmer until the corn is tender. If you use fresh garden corn, you'll hardly have to simmer it at all.

Meanwhile, purée the remaining cup of corn in a blender with some of the stock. You may also blend the milk powder at the same time, or just whisk it into the soup.

Add the purée to the soup pot with the drained beans and salt. Bring the soup almost to boiling, lower the heat, and simmer for a few minutes. Check the seasoning and serve (with a pat of butter on top of each serving, if you like).

Thick Corn and Bean Chowder: Add up to 1 cup of milk powder and 1 or 2 cooked potatoes to the soup.

Noodle Surprise

4 portions

**1 portion = approx. 23 grams of usable protein
53% to 64% of average daily protein need**

The surprise is the crunch of sunflower seeds in a creamy sauce. Add more than half of your daily protein just for eating it!

2 cups whole wheat
   macaroni or other
   whole grain noodles
1 medium onion, chopped
6 large mushrooms,
   chopped
2/3 cup sunflower seeds
3 tbsp oil

1 generous cup grated
   cheese (reserve some
   for the top)
2 eggs, beaten
2/3 cup yogurt
2 pinches cayenne
1 tsp salt
1/2 tsp Worcestershire
   sauce
whole grain bread crumbs

Cook the noodles until tender; drain.

Sauté the onion, mushrooms, and sunflower seeds in the oil until the vegetables are soft and the seeds crisp.

Combine the drained noodles with the sautéed vegetables. Stir in the cheese, eggs, yogurt, and seasonings.

Turn into an oiled casserole, top with bread crumbs and reserved grated cheese.

Bake at 350°F for 30 minutes, until the casserole is firm.

Easy Yogurt Dressing

2 cups

2 cups = approx. 11 grams of usable protein
¼ cup = 3% to 4% of average daily protein need

1½ cups yogurt
2 tsp tamari soy sauce
½ tsp garlic powder*

½ tsp onion powder*
1 tsp celery salt

Stir all of the ingredients together in a small bowl. Serve on tossed greens or other fresh vegetables.

*You may use fresh minced onion and garlic, if desired.

23

Autumn Black Beans

Green Salad
with Mock Thousand Island Dressing

Baked Apple
with Pumpkin Cookies or Bars

Autumn Black Beans

4 small portions

**1 portion = approx. 7 grams of usable protein
16% to 20% of average daily protein need**

A subtle sweet and sour dish of "pudding" consistency.

½ cup dry black beans, cooked tender	I tbsp honey
½ tsp salt	¾ cup yogurt
½ tsp dry mustard	2/3 cup raw bulgur wheat, cooked
I tbsp molasses	raw wheat germ

After the black beans are cooked, drain them and place in a small mixing bowl.

Add the salt, mustard, molasses, and honey. Stir in the yogurt and then the cooked bulgur. Blend carefully to break up any lumps of cooked wheat.

Pour the mixture into a small oiled baking dish, sprinkle with wheat germ, and bake at 350°F for 20 to 25 minutes, until the pudding is firm.

Bulgur with Black Bean Sauce: Instead of stirring the bulgur into the beans, keep it separate and serve the beans and yogurt over it. Sprinkle each portion with wheat germ. This variation is a quicker dish than the original, as there is no baking time.

Mock Thousand Island Dressing

about 1½ cups

**1½ cups = approx. 13 grams of usable protein
¼ cup = 5% to 6% of average daily protein need**

By substituting yogurt for mayonnaise, not only do we increase the protein of Thousand Island Dressing, but we also drastically reduce the calories. A cup of whole milk yogurt has about 160 calories, while a cup of mayonnaise has about 1,750 calories, or 11 times more than the yogurt!!

1 cup yogurt
6 tbsp catsup or
  chili sauce
1 clove garlic, minced
2 tbsp chopped pickle
1 chopped hard-boiled
  egg

2 tbsp chopped scallions
  or chives
2 tbsp chopped green
  olives
1 tsp prepared mustard
1 tsp paprika
1 tbsp Worcestershire
  sauce

Combine all ingredients in the order given.

Keep refrigerated, and eat with eggs and tomatoes or plain lettuce.

Pumpkin Cookies or Bars

2 dozen cookies

**2 cookies = approx. 3 grams of usable protein
7% to 8% of average daily protein need**

Substitute yams or other winter squash for the pumpkin if you want to.

1¼ cups whole wheat
   flour
5 tbsp soy flour
1 tsp baking soda
½ tsp salt
½ tsp cinnamon
½ tsp nutmeg
¼ tsp cloves

½ cup butter
2/3 cup honey
1 egg
1 cup cooked and
   puréed pumpkin
1 cup chopped walnuts
½ cup chopped raisins
½ cup chopped dates

Stir together the dry ingredients and spices.

In another bowl cream the butter and honey; beat in the egg until the mixture is smooth. Stir in the pumpkin purée, and don't worry if the texture is strange.

Add the dry ingredients to the pumpkin mixture; blend, then stir in the nuts and dried fruit.

Drop by heaping tablespoons onto an oiled cookie sheet.

Bake at 325°F for 15 minutes, until they are golden.

Pumpkin Bars: Pour the cookie batter into an oiled 8x8-inch pan. Bake at 350°F for 25 minutes. Cool and cut into squares.

24

Macaroni and Beans
Sweet and Sour Cabbage
Baked Custard

Macaroni and Beans

4 portions

**1 portion = approx. 18 grams of usable protein
42% to 50% of average daily protein need**

This dish is an interesting and spicy blend. No one
would ever guess there were soybeans in it! It's a
quickie, too.

1½ cups dry whole wheat
   macaroni, cooked until
   tender
1 cup chopped onions
1–2 cloves crushed or
   minced garlic
1 cup chopped
   mushrooms (optional)
½–¾ cups stock
2 tsp oregano

½ cup dry soybeans,
   cooked until soft, then
   puréed with a small
   amount of stock
1 cup yogurt
½ cup sesame seeds,
   ground and roasted
   (see p. 134)
Parmesan cheese
   (optional)

While the macaroni is cooking, sauté the onions,
garlic, and optional mushrooms in a small amount of oil
until the onions are soft. Pour in ½ cup stock and add
the oregano. Simmer the mixture 5 to 10 minutes until
the oregano is very fragrant and has softened completely. Add more stock if the mixture becomes too
dry. Turn the onion sauté into a saucepan (2½ quarts
should be big enough).

Stir the puréed soybeans into the sauté, then add the
macaroni. Simmer the mixture until it is at serving
temperature.

Remove it from the heat and stir in the yogurt, which
will make it creamy.

You may next EITHER stir in the sesame seed meal
OR turn the prepared dish onto a serving platter and

sprinkle the sesame meal over all. (Stir in or sprinkle the Parmesan cheese as well—your choice!)

Variation: In reference to the last step above: If you are interested in making the dish a little more elegant, and your oven happens to be on, sprinkle on first the sesame meal, then the Parmesan cheese, dot with butter, and heat in the oven until the dish is bubbly.

Barley, Rye, Millet, Oats, Wheat

Sweet and Sour Cabbage

8 portions

**1 portion = approx. 7 grams of usable protein
17% to 20% of average daily protein need**

This dish has the tang of sweet and sour, but is especially unusual because of the caraway flavor. It might be a side dish at a big feast, but it is delicious enough all by itself for a one-course meal.

1/2 head of a large
    cabbage, shredded
2 medium onions,
    chopped
juice of 2 lemons
4 apples, diced—about
    2 cups (optional)
1/4 cup apple cider
    vinegar
1/4 cup oil

1/4 cup honey
1 tbsp crushed caraway
    seeds
1/2 cup raisins
1/8 tsp allspice
1 cup cottage cheese
1 1/2 cups raw bulgur
    wheat
1 cup yogurt

Combine all ingredients *except* the yogurt.

Place in an oiled casserole and bake covered at 350°F for about 30 minutes, until the bulgur is tender. Place a dab of yogurt on each portion.

Note: When I first mixed up the ingredients for the cabbage dish, several of us started eating it raw. Try it raw and add the cooked bulgur or other cooked grain for a wonderful salad.

Baked Custard

5 small portions

**1 portion = approx. 6 grams of usable protein
14% to 17% of average daily protein need**

Any custard recipe with milk and eggs is a good protein dessert—light, nourishing, and delicious. It is particularly good with the rich combination of the Macaroni and Beans and Sweet and Sour Cabbage.

2 cups milk plus 2 tbsp
   powdered milk (or 3
   tbsp instant)
2 eggs, well beaten

2–4 tbsp honey
1 tsp vanilla (or other
   flavoring—see below)

Beat the powdered milk into the whole milk OR you may use all powdered milk and water.

Beat the eggs into the milk with a wire whisk; add the honey and vanilla.

Pour the mixture into lightly oiled or buttered custard cups, or one baking dish. Place in a pan of hot water filled halfway up the sides of the cups or dish.

Bake at 325°F for about 50 minutes, until a knife inserted in the center comes out clean.

Other Flavors:

1. Add 2 tsp rum or brandy to the basic recipe, and omit the vanilla.

2. Add 1 tbsp carob powder to the basic recipe.

3. Add a few drops peppermint extract; omit the vanilla.

4. Add a few drops almond extract; omit the vanilla.

5. Stir in ¼ to ½ cup lightly toasted unsweetened coconut. Add ½ cup chocolate or carob chips, too.

Cows

25

Hot Cheese Soup
Very Brown Rice
Green Beans, Steamed
Crunchy Nut Muffins

Hot Cheese Soup

about 1½ quarts

**1 cup = approx. 21 grams of usable protein
49% to 59% of average daily protein need**

This soup is decidedly spicy. If you are not fond of chilies, omit them and the soup will be mild. It's a filling soup, but it sparks the appetite, so it's an ideal first course.

2 tbsp butter
¼ cup minced onion
¼ cup finely chopped carrots
¼ cup finely chopped celery
¼ cup finely chopped red or green sweet peppers
2 tbsp minced hot green chili peppers
¼ cup whole wheat flour

5 cups stock (or stock and wine)
½ cup sesame tahini or sesame butter
½ pound cheddar (or other soft cheese), grated—about 2 cups
6 tbsp milk powder (½ cup instant)
1 tsp salt
1¼ cups toasted sunflower seeds

Melt the butter in a large soup pot; sauté the onions, carrots, celery, green peppers, and hot peppers until all the vegetables are soft, but not brown.

Stir in the whole wheat flour and heat for 1 minute; add the stock and bring the mixture to a boil.

Use a whisk to blend in the tahini (which will look curdled). Lower the heat and simmer for five minutes.

Add the cheese by handfuls, whisking until each one has melted completely. Carefully whisk in the milk powder (or use a blender to buzz it with 1 cup of the soup).

Add the salt, and just before serving stir in the sunflower seeds.

Very Brown Rice

8 portions

**1 portion = approx. 6 grams of usable protein
13% to 16% of average daily protein need**

Serve with a steamed vegetable or a salad.

1/4 cup oil
2 cups raw brown rice
2 tbsp butter, divided
    into small chunks
4 1/2 or 5 1/2–6 cups water,
    for pressure cooking or
    regular cooking,
    respectively

3/4 cup dry mixed small
    beans, such as mung,
    split peas, red, or lentils
    (soaked for regular
    cooking; see p. 132)
2 tsp salt

Heat the oil in a large saucepan or pressure cooker.

Add the rice and sauté it for 5 to 7 minutes, until it crackles and browns lightly.

Stir in the chunks of butter until they melt; then add the water and mixed beans.

Pressure cook for 15 minutes. For regular cooking, cook until the rice and beans are tender, adding more water if necessary.

Stir in the salt and serve.

Crunchy Nut Muffins

about 16 muffins

**2 muffins = approx. 8 grams of usable protein
17% to 21% of average daily protein need**

These muffins are a perfect accompaniment to soup and salad. Toast the leftovers and spread with ricotta cheese.

1½ cups whole wheat flour	¼ cup chopped and toasted peanuts
¼ cup soy flour	1/3 cup currants or raisins
1 tbsp baking powder	1 egg, beaten
½ tsp salt	1 cup milk
¼ cup toasted sesame seeds	1–4 tbsp melted butter or oil
1/3 cup toasted sunflower seeds	1–4 tbsp honey

Stir all of the dry ingredients together. This should include the seeds, nuts, and raisins.

In a separate bowl beat the egg; add the milk, butter or oil, honey, and blend.

Make a well in the dry ingredients and add the liquid mixture all at once. Stir just enough to moisten the dry ingredients.

Drop the batter into well-oiled muffin tins. Bake at 375°F for 15 to 20 minutes. And serve them hot.

Nutty Nut Muffins: For an even nuttier muffin, add up to 1½ cups more chopped peanuts. The milk will complement them.

26

Peanut, Tofu, and Sesame Soup

Potato Corn Cakes
with Mushroom and Onion Sauce

Elegant Yogurt Compote

Peanut, Tofu, and Sesame Soup

about 2 quarts

1 cup = approx. 7 grams of usable protein
17% to 20% of average daily protein need

¾ cup raw peanuts,
   cooked
6 ounces tofu, cut in
   ½-inch cubes
¼ cup chopped celery
¾ cup chopped onions
½–1 cup chopped
   mushrooms
4 cups liquid from cooking
   the peanuts

2 cups canned tomatoes
   with some juice
⅞ cup ground and roasted
   sesame seeds (see p.
   134)
1 tbsp miso (soybean
   paste)
2 tsp salt
¼ tsp dried chili peppers
1 bay leaf (remove when
   soup is cooked)

Spread the cooked peanuts on a large cutting board and chop them coarsely. Set aside.

Using a small amount of oil, sauté the tofu cubes with the celery, onions, and mushrooms. The tofu should brown lightly and the onions should be golden.

Combine the sautéed vegetables with the chopped peanuts in a large soup pot or saucepan. Stir in the peanut stock, tomatoes, and the roasted sesame seeds.

Bring the soup to a simmer. Then dissolve the miso in a small amount of the broth and return it to the pot.

Season with salt, chili peppers, and bay leaf. Simmer covered 20 to 25 minutes OR pressure cook for 3 minutes.

Potato Corn Cakes

about 20 cakes

2 cakes = approx. 6 grams of usable protein
14% to 16% of average daily protein need

These cakes are delicious with applesauce and yogurt. You may think that grating the potatoes and onion is a bother, but I'm convinced that grated vegetables make much lighter pancakes.

4 medium potatoes,
  scrubbed, with skins
1 large onion
2 eggs, beaten
1 tbsp brewer's yeast
1 tsp salt

2 tbsp whole wheat flour
1 tbsp soy grits
1 cup milk powder
  (1-1/3 cups instant)
2 cups corn, fresh, frozen,
  or drained canned

Grate the potatoes and the onion (and please leave the potato skins on); stir in the eggs, brewer's yeast, salt, flour, and soy grits.

Carefully add the milk powder so that it doesn't lump too much (a few lumps don't matter).

Stir in the corn, and your cakes are ready to fry.

Fry on an oiled griddle, browning them well on each side. Serve them piping hot with the sauce below.

Mushroom and Onion Sauce

about 4½ cups

4½ cups = approx. 55 grams of usable protein
¼ cup = 7% to 9% of average daily protein need

This sauce was such a hit that I caught a friend heaping it on her plate and eating it straight!

2 tbsp butter
2 tbsp oil
1 cup finely chopped
onions
2 cups mushroom slices
¼ cup whole wheat flour

3 cups milk (hot if
possible)
1 tsp salt (more to taste)
¼ tsp cayenne pepper
(less to taste)
1 cup ricotta cheese

Heat the butter and oil together in a 2-quart saucepan. Sauté the onions and mushrooms until the onions are transparent.

Gradually stir in the whole wheat flour, stirring constantly so that it coats the vegetables. Cook this mixture over gentle heat for about one minute, stirring all the while.

Add the milk, one cup at a time. Simmer the mixture until it has thickened slightly. Add the salt and cayenne while you simmer.

Stir up the ricotta until it is separated and soft. You can even put it in the blender if you're up to it, but it isn't necessary. Add the cheese to the sauce and use a whisk to break up any lumps. The sauce is ready when it's all hot.

Elegant Yogurt Compote

about 1½ quarts

1 cup = approx. 4 grams of usable protein
10% to 12% of average daily protein need

This is an example of how easily you can make an elegant dessert from your own fresh yogurt. Try serving the compote in cream-puff shells, with cookies or cake.

2½ cups plain yogurt,
  preferably homemade
  fresh yogurt
1/3 cup honey
1 cup toasted
  unsweetened coconut
2 cups sliced apricots
(fresh, soaked-dried, or
  home canned)
1 cup grated apples
2–3 drops almond extract
1 cup broken walnuts (or
  other nuts)

Stir the ingredients together in the order given. You may reserve part of the toasted coconut to sprinkle on each individual serving.

Chill several hours before serving.

Sesame seed, flower and pod

27

Garbanzo and Cheese Loaf

Green Salad
with Easy Roquefort Dressing

Fresh Fruit
with Kitchen Sink Cookies

Garbanzo and Cheese Loaf

6 portions

**1 portion = approx. 11 grams of usable protein
25% to 30% of average daily protein need**

The texture is light and crunchy. Try this loaf tomorrow for a sandwich spread.

1 cup whole grain bread crumbs	1/4 cup chopped parsley
1 cup pineapple juice	1 egg, beaten
1/2 cup dry garbanzo beans, cooked tender and drained	1 tbsp miso (soybean paste)
1 cup chopped onion	1 tsp salt
1/2 cup chopped celery	a few dashes hot sauce
3 tbsp oil	2 pinches cayenne
	1 cup grated cheese (try hot pepper and Swiss)

Combine the bread crumbs and pineapple juice and let them soak while you prepare the vegetables.

Either chop the garbanzos coarsely or grind them in a food grinder using the coarse blade. Don't purée them in a blender, because you want them to maintain their nutty texture.

Combine the garbanzos, the crumb mixture, and all the remaining ingredients in the order given. Make sure you dissolve the miso in a small amount of hot water so it doesn't stay in a lump.

Turn the mixture into an oiled loaf pan or small casserole. Bake at 350°F about 40 minutes, until the edges are nicely browned.

Easy Roquefort Dressing

about 1 cup

1 cup = approx. 17 grams usable protein
¼ cup = 10% to 12% of average daily
protein need

6 tbsp yogurt
3 tbsp mayonnaise
3 tbsp cottage cheese

3 tbsp crumbled
Roquefort cheese

Blend all ingredients in a blender until smooth. Use this dressing on any type of salad. It is especially nice on plain lettuce leaves.

Cheeses

Kitchen Sink Cookies

4 dozen cookies

2 cookies = approx. 3 grams of usable protein
6% to 7% of average daily protein need

These delicious cookies contain all those wonderful things that cookies should have!

1 cup whole wheat flour
1/4 cup soy flour
1-1/3 cups rolled oats
3/4 cup unsweetened grated coconut
1/4 cup milk powder (1/3 cup instant)
1/2 tsp salt
1 tsp cinnamon
1/2 tsp powdered ginger

2/3 cup raisins
2/3 cup chocolate chips
1/4 cup chopped peanuts
1/3 cup sunflower seeds
2 eggs, beaten
1/4 cup oil or melted butter
1/4 cup molasses
1/4 cup honey

Stir together all of the dry ingredients (*i.e.*, everything except the eggs, oil, honey, and molasses).

Beat the eggs in a small bowl; measure the oil, then the honey and molasses in the same measuring cup. Beat all the liquid ingredients together thoroughly.

Pour the liquid into the dry ingredients and combine until the dry ingredients are moistened. If the mixture seems too dry add some milk or water until the dough is of drop cookie consistency.

Drop the cookies onto an unoiled cookie sheet. Bake at 350°F for 10 to 12 minutes.

Oatmeal Cookies: Omit the 2/3 cup chocolate chips and you will have delicious oatmeal cookies.

28

Soybean Croquettes
Green Beans with Mushrooms
Indian Pudding with Yogurt Topping

Soybean Croquettes

4 portions

**1 portion = approx. 14 grams of usable protein
32% to 39% of average daily protein need**

1/3 cup dry soybeans (soaked overnight)	1 onion, cut in large chunks for blender or minced by hand
1 onion, chopped	2 tsp butter
1 bay leaf	2 eggs, well beaten
1 tsp salt	bread crumbs or raw wheat germ
2 tomatoes, peeled, seeded, and chopped	
1/4 cup peanuts	3/4 cup raw brown rice
3/4 cup walnuts	2/3 cup raw bulgur wheat

Bean mixture: EITHER: Cook soaked beans* with the chopped onion, bay leaf, and salt, adding tomatoes in the last 10 minutes of cooking; OR: pressure cook unsoaked beans* with bay leaf and onion. Add slightly stewed tomatoes to cooked beans. Drain liquid (save for future soups). Mash slightly.

Nut mixture: EITHER: Blend together in an electric blender peanuts, walnuts, cut-up onion, and butter just until nuts are ground; OR: grind nuts in a mortar and blend by hand with minced onion and butter. Combine the bean and nut mixtures. Combination should be quite moist but if *too* moist add bread crumbs. Form into balls, dip in egg, and roll in wheat germ or bread crumbs. Bake at 400°F until brown, about 30 minutes. Serve on a bed of rice and bulgur that have been prepared according to the sauté method.† Pour a cheese sauce, Italian tomato sauce, or any favorite sauce over

---

*See Basic Cooking Instructions, page 132.
†See Basic Cooking Instructions, page 134.

the croquettes and grains, and you have an elegant dish. Serve with a green vegetable.

Indian Pudding

4 to 6 portions

**1 portion = approx. 12 grams of usable protein
28% to 34% of average daily protein need**

4 cups milk
1 cup yellow cornmeal
1/4 cup soy grits soaked in
 1/2 cup water
1/3 cup butter (fill a cup
 2/3 full of water, then
 add butter till cup is
 brimming; drain off
 water)

1/2 cup brown sugar
2/3 cup light molasses
3/4 tsp salt
1/2 tsp cinnamon
1/4 tsp ground cloves
1/4 tsp ginger
1/8 tsp allspice
1/8 tsp nutmeg
2 eggs, beaten

Bring milk to a boil, add cornmeal and soy grits gradually, stirring all the while. Lower heat and beat with a wire whisk to maintain a smooth mixture. When mixture begins to thicken remove from heat. Add remaining ingredients *except* eggs and allow to cool slightly. Blend in the beaten eggs, pour into a buttered baking dish, and bake 45 to 60 minutes in a 325°F oven, or until pudding is firm.

This pudding is delicious both hot and cold, especially with yogurt, sour cream, or ice cream. For a variation you may add 1/2 cup dried fruits and omit the brown sugar.

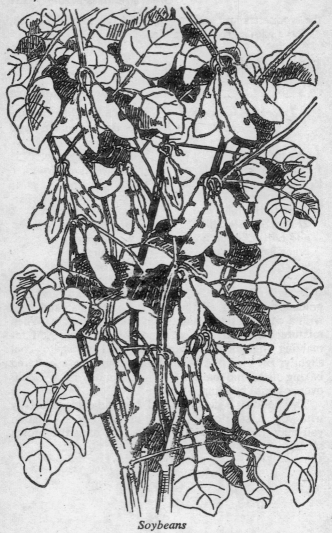

Soybeans

9

Savory Onion Quiche

Tabouli

Tangy Rice–Sesame Pudding

Savory Onion Quiche

two 9-inch pies (12 portions)

**1 portion = approx. 12 grams of usable protein
28% to 34% of average daily protein need**

Pastry shell:

1½ cups whole wheat
 flour
½ cup soy flour
½ tsp salt

¼ cup oil
1 tbsp poppy seeds
ice water

Mix dry ingredients and oil with a pastry blender or fork. Add just enough ice water to make a firm dough. Roll out and put into two oiled 9-inch pie pans and chill.

Filling:

3 cups onions, chopped
 and sautéed
2½ cups grated cheese
3 cups milk

½ cup instant milk powder
4–5 eggs
1 tsp salt
½ tsp thyme

Spread the onions over the two pie shells and cover with the cheese. Blend the milk, milk powder, eggs, salt, and thyme and pour over the cheese. Bake at 350°F for 25 to 30 minutes until firm.

A superb supper dish, this quiche is especially good with strong cheese like Port-Salut and St. Paulin mixed with some hot pepper cheese. (When I don't have hot pepper cheese, I like to substitute a tablespoon of finely minced green chilies.) If using only mild cheeses, add a dash of Worcestershire sauce and ½ tsp dry mustard.

Tabouli
Zesty Lebanese Salad

6 portions

1 portion = approx. 4 grams of usable protein
9% to 11% of average daily protein need

1¼ cups raw bulgur wheat
4 cups boiling water
¼ cup dry white or garbanzo beans, cooked and drained
1½ cups minced parsley*
¾ cup minced mint* (if not available, substitute more parsley)
¾ cup minced scallions

3 medium tomatoes, chopped
¾ cup lemon juice
¼ cup olive oil
1–2 tsp salt
freshly ground pepper to taste
raw grape, lettuce, or cabbage leaves

Pour the boiling water over the bulgur and let stand about 2 hours until the wheat is light and fluffy. Drain excess water and shake in a strainer or press with hands to remove as much water as possible. Mix the bulgur, cooked beans, and remaining ingredients. Chill for at least 1 hour. Serve on raw leaves.

This recipe is adapted from a traditional Lebanese dish often served on festive occasions. If you want to be truly authentic, let your guests or family scoop it up with lettuce leaves instead of using spoons. A Lebanese friend once served tabouli as a party hors d'oeuvre. It was a great hit.

---

*You can use the blender. A wooden chopstick is good for scraping the leaves from the sides of the blender into the blade action.

Tangy Rice–Sesame Pudding

6 portions

**1 portion = approx. 6 grams of usable protein
14% to 17% of average daily protein need**

¾ cup raw brown rice,
  cooked
2–2½ cups orange juice
6 tbsp sesame meal
2/3 cup brown sugar,
  packed
grated rind of one orange
  (can use blender)

4 eggs, well beaten
½ tsp each cinnamon and
  ginger
¼ tsp nutmeg
1 tsp vanilla extract
½ cup raisins (optional)

Combine all the ingredients well. Place in oiled baking dish and bake at 350°F for 1 hour, or until firm. Especially good served warm.

30

Creamy Mushroom Soup
Soy–Peanut Marinade
Spiced Fruit Rice Pudding

Creamy Mushroom Soup

about 3 quarts

1 cup = approx. 5 grams of usable protein
12% to 15% of average daily protein need

7 tbsp butter
3 tbsp oil
1½ cups chopped onions
3 cups chopped
  mushroom stems
1 cup hot water (or stock)
3 medium potatoes, about
  4 cups, diced small
5 cups hot stock

4 cups sliced
  mushroom caps
2 tsp salt
¼ tsp paprika
¼ cup dry white wine
1½ cups milk powder
  (2 cups instant)
¼ cup or more chopped
  parsley

Melt 3 tablespoons of the butter and 2 tablespoons of the oil in a large soup pot. Sauté the onions and mushroom stems for about 15 minutes, until the onions are transparent and begin to brown. Stir in the 1 cup water or stock and simmer for 10 minutes. Put the mixture into a blender and buzz until it's completely smooth. Set the purée aside.

Melt 2 tablespoons of the butter and the remaining tablespoon of oil in the same soup pot. Add the potatoes and sauté them over low heat, stirring for about 7 minutes until they become translucent. Stir in the mushroom–onion purée and 5 cups hot stock. Bring the mixture to a boil, lower the heat, cover, and simmer for 15 minutes, stirring occasionally.

In a small frying pan sauté the sliced mushroom caps in the remaining 2 tablespoons of butter until they are soft.

Stir the salt and paprika into the soup pot along with the sautéed cap slices, and the wine.

Simmer the soup while you mix the milk powder with a small amount of water to make a paste. Add this to the soup and simmer a few more minutes while you check the seasoning. Sprinkle the parsley over each serving of soup.

Mushrooms

Soy–Peanut Marinade

4 portions

**1 portion = approx. 19 grams of usable protein
45% to 54% of average daily protein need**

Refreshing on a summer day . . .

1 cup raw peanuts, cooked
½ cup soybeans, cooked
¼ cup honey
¼ cup apple cider vinegar
2 tbsp sesame oil
¼ cup sesame tahini or sesame butter

½ tsp salt
¼ tsp dry mustard
¼ tsp dry tarragon
1–2 tbsp chopped parsley
½ onion, sliced into thin rings
2/3 cup sesame seeds, toasted (see p. 134)

After the beans are cooked, drain them well.
Combine the honey, vinegar, oil, tahini, salt, herbs, and spices, through the parsley.
Toss the dressing into the cooked peanuts and beans;

add the onion rings, cover, and chill several hours or overnight.

Just before serving stir in the sesame seeds and transfer the marinade to a bowl lined with greens.

Spiced Fruit Rice Pudding

6 portions

**1 portion = approx. 9 grams of usable protein
20% to 24% of average daily protein need**

A rice pudding with a difference . . .

1½ cups raw brown rice	¼ tsp ginger
2½ or 3 cups milk	2 tbsp lemon juice
pinch of salt	2 cups coarsely chopped
½ cup honey	fruit—fresh or soaked
1 egg, beaten	dried apples, apricots,
½ tsp cinnamon	or oranges
½ tsp nutmeg	1 cup yogurt

Cook the rice in a pressure cooker or regular saucepan, using milk instead of water. Use 2½ cups milk in the pressure cooker OR 3 cups for regular cooking.

When cooked, the rice should be tender but it will look soupier than rice cooked with water. Stir in the honey, egg, cinnamon, nutmeg, and ginger.

Oil a 1-quart casserole and spread half the rice mixture over the bottom. Sprinkle lemon juice over the fruits and gently place half of them on top of the rice. Repeat the two layers and place in a 350°F oven.

Bake the pudding for 25 minutes. Remove from the oven and spread the 1 cup yogurt over the top. Chill several hours before serving.

Basic Cooking Instructions

Beans, Grains, Nuts, and Seeds

In order to avoid repetition among the recipes, here are instructions for preparing the basic ingredients often called for. The recipes usually give the *raw* measure for grains and beans (*i.e.,* "1 cup raw brown rice, cooked"); you should then cook that amount of grain with the appropriate amount of water, milk, or stock. If you have a supply of cooked grain or beans in the refrigerator, you should measure more than the amount specified in the raw measure, as follows:

Most grains, including rice:
   1 cup raw equals about 3 cups cooked
Millet and buckwheat:
   1 cup raw equals about 4 cups cooked
Beans:
   1 cup raw equals about 4 to 5 cups cooked.

Cooking Beans
1. Regular cooking: Wash beans in cold water, and soak overnight in three times the volume of water; *or* bring the beans and water to a boil, cover tightly, and let sit for 2 hours. Simmer the beans, partially covered, adding water if necessary, for about 2 hours, depending on the type of bean and the consistency you want. If you want to mash or purée the beans, you will want to cook them until they are quite soft.

2. Pressure cooking: A pressure cooker is a real advantage in cooking beans as well as grains. Since the foods cook so much more quickly, a meal doesn't require as much forethought! Pressure cooking also gives you a tenderer bean. Soaking or precooking, as in method 1, saves a little time, but with pressure cooking it really is not necessary. Bring the washed beans and three to four times their volume in water to a boil in the cooker. Cover and bring to 15 pounds pressure. Cook beans for 25 to 45 minutes. Cool immediately. Don't attempt to cook split peas or any bean that tends to foam in a pressure cooker, or you may find yourself with a clogged cooker and a big mess.

3. Roasting: Cook beans by one of the above methods for a firm bean. Then spread the beans on a lightly oiled baking sheet. Sprinkle with salt, if desired, and bake at 200°F for about 1 hour until they are well browned. When they are hot, they will be crunchy outside and tender inside. When they are cool they will be hard and crunchy throughout. You can also roast the beans in a lightly oiled frying pan over medium heat on top of the stove. Stir constantly. Roasted soybeans can be eaten alone whole; when chopped, or ground in a blender, they make a garnish to be sprinkled on a variety of dishes. Also use them when nuts or nutmeal is called for.

4. Making soybean curd (tofu): Soybean curd can be purchased in many parts of the country. If it is not available to you, you might wish to try making it. *The Natural Foods Cookbook* has several recipes. I'm not including a recipe here because my single attempt failed. However, the "failure" served as a base for a delicious salad dressing made by blending spices, herbs, onions, garlic, and avocado.

Cooking Grains

1. Regular cooking: Wash the grains in cold water. Bring stock or water, equal to twice the volume of the grains, to a boil (for millet or buckwheat use three times the volume). Put in the grains, bring to a boil again, lower heat and simmer (covered) for 30 to 45 minutes, until all of the liquid is absorbed.

2. Pressure cooking: In the pressure cooker follow

the same method, but instead of simmering the grain, bring to 15 pounds pressure and cook for about 20 minutes. Cool under cold water when the cooking time is up. You may wish to vary the amount of water to create the texture of grain you prefer. If you have trouble with sticking, here's the trick I use: Place about 1 inch of water in the bottom of the pressure cooker. Put the grain into a stainless steel bowl that will fit easily into the pressure cooker (with plenty of room between the top of the bowl and the lid of the pressure cooker). Add water to the level of about ¾ inch above the level of the grain. Put the bowl inside the pressure cooker, cover, and begin cooking. This method is also handy when I need to cook both grains and beans at the same time, but separately. I merely put the small stainless steel bowl inside the pressure cooker. I then place the beans with adequate water around the outside of the bowl and the grains inside the bowl.

3. *Sautéeing:* This method is most frequently used in cooking bulgur wheat and buckwheat groats, but can be used with any grain to achieve a "nuttier" flavor. Wash the grains and put in a dry saucepan or pressure cooker over low heat. Stir until dry. Add just enough oil to coat each kernel. Sauté the grains, stirring constantly, until all of the grains are golden. Stir in boiling water or stock (amounts given in 1 above) and bring the mixture to a boil. Cover and simmer 30 to 45 minutes; or, if using a pressure cooker, bring to 15 pounds pressure and cook 20 minutes. Cool cooker immediately.

Cooking Nuts and Seeds

1. *To roast whole seeds or nuts:* Place in a dry pan and roast over medium flame until desired brownness. Or spread them on a baking sheet and toast them in a 200°F oven. Use the seeds whole, or grind them in a blender, a few at a time, or with a mortar and pestle. Add salt if desired.

2. *To roast or toast seed or nut meal:* Buy the meal,

or, to make it yourself, grind the seeds or nuts in a blender. Then roast the meal in a dry pan, stirring constantly, adding salt, if desired. Or spread the meal on a baking sheet, and bake at 200°F, stirring often. (You can also grind small quantities of whole grains in your blender.)

3. *Nut and seed butters:* It is easy to make your own fresh nut and seed butters if you have a blender. From whole roasted or raw seeds or nuts: Grind as for meal, adding a little oil to "start" the butter. Continue adding as many nuts or seeds as your blender can handle. From roasted or raw nut or seed meal: Stir a little oil, and honey, if desired, into the meal, and you will have creamy nut or seed butter.

Stock

A word about stock: A stock pot is a basic necessity for nutritious cooking. Any leftover vegetables and the liquid in which they were cooked should go into the refrigerated stock pot. If you're caught without any stock, you can quickly make good, nutritious stock by simmering lettuce leaves, carrot tops, bits of onion— practically any vegetable trimmings—briefly in a quart of water.

Whole Wheat Pie Crust

two 9-inch single crusts

**when complemented with dairy products,
1 crust = approx. 14 grams of usable protein**

This crust is a plain whole wheat crust that you can use for quiches or sweet cheese desserts. Any dairy product or even a bean pie will complement it.

2 cups whole wheat pastry flour	1/2 cup soft shortening
1/2 tsp salt	about 1/2 cup water

Stir the whole wheat pastry flour and salt together.

Work the shortening in with a knife or pastry blender, but don't work it in too much. The pieces may be quite lumpy, but it will make a flakier crust.

Add about 1/3 cup of water and move the crust mixture around so the water will soak in. Gather the dough gently and add more water if there is some flour that won't gather.

Divide the dough in half, roll each half and fit into pie plates OR you may use half of the crust for an upper crust.

If you are making an unbaked pie, bake the crust at 375°F for 10 to 15 minutes. Prick the bottom with a fork so it will stay flat OR put about 1/4 cup of raw rice over the bottom to hold the crust down.

Index

5 of the best reasons to eat nutritiously.